SEVEN FRENCH CHRONICLERS

SEVEN FRENCH CHRONICLERS

Witnesses to History

Paul Archambault

SYRACUSE UNIVERSITY PRESS
1974

Copyright © 1974 by Syracuse University Press, Syracuse, New York
ALL RIGHTS RESERVED
FIRST EDITION

Library of Congress Cataloging in Publication Data

Archambault, Paul, 1937–
    Seven French chroniclers.

    Bibliography: p.
    1. France—Historiography.   2. Middle Ages—
Historiography.   I. Title.
DC36.9.A64   907'.202'2   73-16652
ISBN 0-8156-0099-2

95190

Manufactured in the United States of America

For Laura and Nicholas Joost

Paul Archambault is professor of French at Syracuse University and is currently resident director of its University of Strasbourg study program. The author of *Camus' Hellenic Sources* and journal articles, Archambault received the B.A. degree from Assumption College and the Ph.D. from Yale University.

CONTENTS

PREFACE

THE medieval chronicler was an interested and partisan witness not only to the events of his time but to its tastes, prejudices, and preferences as to what was visually and perceptually significant. More than a mere scribe who contented himself with recording dates, facts, and gossip, the chronicler endowed his narrative with an intense view of the world and a projection on the world of acquired and often unconscious perceptual modes.

This book considers seven French chroniclers of the late Middle Ages and watches them in the highly subjective act of looking at their world. It approaches a type of literature traditionally read for its documentary or esthetic interest and asks of it untraditional questions. How does this chronicler look (in the most literal sense of that word) at the world about him? How does the world about him look, as reflected or refracted by his vision? Is his sense of importance characteristic of the thought of his age? Can his modes of perception be considered both as products of his cultural milieu and as means of transmitting it? More broadly, does this chronicler order his perception according to an implicit structure or sense of history? How does he reconstruct his world?

There is something arbitrary about any choice; and if pressed to explain why I chose these chroniclers rather than any of their contemporaries I should have to reply in the first place that I enjoy reading them more. But my choice was not entirely a matter of personal taste. I also intended at the outset to select representative chroniclers of the late medieval period, both to give my study some historical continuity and to attempt to determine whether there is a shift of focus in the process of late medieval chronicle writing. My concluding chapter suggests the tentative reply that there does not seem to be a discernible evolution in the chroniclers' modes of perception that might necessarily be linked to the events themselves; rather, perceptual modes appear to be a product of the chronicler's personality, and, like personalities, they lend themselves only *a posteriori* to a classification of types.

I have deliberately avoided the Crocean distinction between chronicle and history, and so the words *chronicler* and *historiographer* will be used interchangeably. Some of these chroniclers wrote quite by chance, whether to justify a political or military role they had once played or to vindicate themselves in the eyes of posterity. In some cases, the chronicle was a command performance: someone had approached the chronicler-to-be, asking him for a book of personal memoirs. Some wrote to indulge their literary tastes and needed the subsidy of wealthy patrons. Some were thrust into the position of chronicle writing after fulfilling other social stations. With the exception of Georges Chastellain and Olivier de la Marche, who served as official historiographers for a part of their careers at the Burgundian court, none of the chroniclers under discussion was charged with writing historiography, and each composed his chronicle either by happenstance or by a personal need for justification.

The chroniclers discussed here belong to both literature and history. They might as legitimately be read in Old French literature courses as in seminars on medieval historiography. Even a few years ago, literature and history appeared sealed off from each other; more often than not, their votaries worked in silent and mutually uncommunicative isolation. Academic boundaries seem less clearly delineated nowadays, and scholars with interests both literary and historical seem to take pride in asking themselves cross-disciplinary questions.

This study, then, outlines the structure of reality as it might have appeared to the chroniclers themselves. The chronicler's manner of perceiving and ordering his perception, his selection of details, the conceptual models into which he fits his facts—these problems constitute an essential part of both history and literature. One reader can choose to attune himself to the visual, linguistic, and thematic patterns of a chronicler's record quite as arguably as another might choose to attune himself to the accuracy of his facts. Reading in the former mode might clarify the visual and conceptual habits that contribute to the arrangement of the narrative.

In 1966, the French medieval scholar Paul Rousset criticized historians for being more attentive to the facts the chroniclers reported than to the psychological substance of the facts and the manner in which they were presented. Rousset wrote that modern historians have ignored aspects of history considered essential by their medieval predecessors.

Rousset's criticism is perhaps beginning to lose some of its justification. The mental structures of medieval civilization are proving to be one of its most fertile areas of study. Historians of the French structuralist school like Georges Duby and Jacques Le Goff have concentrated their research on what they currently term the *outillage mental,* the mental equipment, of medieval civilization. Books like Robert Hanning's *The Vision of History in Early Britain* (New York: Columbia University Press, 1966) and William J. Brandt's *The Shape of Medieval History* (New Haven: Yale University Press, 1966) have already demonstrated that chronicle writing in particular can be examined not only for its content but for its presentation and psychological substance. Perhaps more than other genres, chronicle literature might prove a common area of interest for philology, literary history, the history of political and social institutions, and even for the history of psychology. Intellectual, moral, and esthetic modes of perception seem as legitimate an object of historical study as art, economics, or legal theory. For the medieval period, at least, the history of those modes is yet to be written.

Most of Chapter Two appeared originally in *Papers on Language and Literature* VII, 2:115–32, as an article entitled "The Silences of Joinville." Chapter Six is a revised version of an article that also appeared in *PLL* IV, 3 (1968):227–57, under the title "Sallust in France: Thomas Basin's Idea of History and of the Human Condition." Chapter Seven is the revised version of an article printed in *Symposium* XXVII, 1 (1973):5–18. I am grateful to Nicholas Joost, editor of *PLL,* and J. H. Matthews, editor of *Symposium,* for their generous permission to reprint the parts of this book that appeared previously in these journals.

Syracuse, New York   Paul Archambault
September 1973

SEVEN FRENCH CHRONICLERS

1 THE DISINTEGRATION
OF SYSTEMS

The "Universalist" Tradition

Historians, no matter what their underlying convictions, generally agree that the Fathers of the Western Church abandoned the Greek theory of cycles in favor of a linear view of the direction of history that attempted to embrace and give meaning to the entire course of human events. The linear view, however, did not issue full-panoplied from the minds of the early Christian writers. Ever since the conquests of Alexander there existed in the Mediterranean basin the concept of a world conceived as a totality in scope, an *ecuméné*, as opposed to the Greek idea of the *pólis*, the city state. This notion of historical universality—perhaps the first indication of the one-world idea in the ancient world—was promoted by the vast geographical expansion of the Hellenistic world. Ethically it was reflected by the Stoic ideas, prevalent around the beginning of the Christian era, which asserted that the barriers between Greek and barbarian no longer existed, that man is brother to man, and that the real home of the Stoic philosopher is not the city but the world. Roman historians of the imperial age—Lucius Annaeus Florus, Flavius Vopiscus, Ammianus Marcellinus—had attempted to interpret and give meaning to the entire course of human history; each had implicitly or explicitly compared the rise and decline of the Roman empire to the infancy, adolescence, manhood, and old age of man; each had imagined the decline of Rome as beginning with, or immediately before, the reign of Augustus; for each of them, the manhood of Rome had been characterized by military and moral strength; each of them thought of Roman history as coextensive with the history of the world. The "orbis terrarum," as it had risen, developed, and declined, was a unique phenomenon in time: it might renew itself, it might not die im-

1

mediately, but it would never repeat itself in the same way. None of the Roman historians would have claimed, like Aristotle, to be living at the same time as the Trojan war. There had been brave men before Agamemnon, as Horace had said; but none of Horace's contemporaries would have maintained that their age was the same as that of the Homeric heroes.

The idea of a linear and ecumenical theory of historical development, often thought to be an Augustinian or medieval invention, was in fact transmitted by the Roman historians to the Church Fathers. Christian writers of the first three centuries—Hippolytus of Rome, Tertullian, Cyprian—were familiar with the attempts made by their pagan predecessors, principally the Roman historians, to draw analogies between the development of man and that of the world. To these attempts they added their own. For the classical Roman notion of the history of the empire, they substituted the idea of the history of salvation. And whenever they discussed the history of salvation they invariably looked upon it as an irreversible, universal progression toward a goal. This progression had already traversed a succession of ages. Christian writers of the early centuries remembered St. Paul's fourfold classification of the historical ages: law of Nature, Mosaic law, age of Grace, age of Glory. The Old Testament, to which the Church Fathers were so indebted for their vision of history, was a historical document containing an evident universal significance and an equally evident idea of progression. Some of the New Testament parables provided the Fathers with yet other schemes according to which the successive ages of history might be serialized. The story of the Master's appearance at three successive vigils of night (Luke XII:38) might signify three stages of God's revelation in history, or in the life of each man. The parable of the laborers in the vineyard arriving for work at five different hours of the day (Matthew XX:1–19) might suggest a five-fold division of the history of salvation.[1]

The habit of using chronological systems so as better to comprehend and serialize the events of universal history was part of the heritage passed on from Roman to early Christian historiography. No single system or model was ever used by any of the Christian writers to the exclusion of another; but any model that became part of the Christian historiographical tradition had some characteristic points about it. It used Scripture as its basic historical reference. The ages of the history of salvation might or might not encompass the history of the great pagan empires—the Persian, the Babylonian, the Greek, the Roman—but the milestones of history were definitely biblical: the ages of the world were delimited by figures like Adam, Noah, Abraham, and David. And whether the Christian writer chose to construct his system from a text of Genesis, Daniel, or Saint Paul, the structure of his system was always linear. The system might be based on the model of a straight line, of an ascending line, even of converging lines; it could never be represented by a curve or a circle.

The medieval tradition of universal chronicle writing based upon Scripturally inspired systems originates especially with Eusebius and Augustine. Eusebius of Caesarea (ca. A.D. 261–338), whose *Ecclesiastical History* is the foundation of all medieval universal histories, provided medieval historiography with its first all-embracing Christian view of history.[2] The apologetic intention of Eusebius' historical works need not concern us here. What is important is that he was the first Christian writer to adopt an ecumenical view of biblical as well as profane history and to attempt to frame it within a chronological system whose basic structure is a succession of points. The presence of this word *succession* (*diadoché*) in the opening sentence of his *Ecclesiastical History* marks its importance in Eusebius' system: "The chief matters to be dealt with in this work are the following: . . . the lines of succession from the holy apostles, and the periods that have elapsed from our Saviour's time to our own."[3]

Augustine's chronological system, though structurally linear like that of Eusebius, was both more complex and more widely used. The Augustinian system seems to consist of an interweaving of three biblical models, each based on the number seven: the seven ages of man, the seven days of Creation, the seven biblical periods between Adam and the second coming of Christ. In the *De Genesi contra Manichaeos,* and again in the *De Civitate Dei,* Augustine coordinates his threefold model into a coherent system. The first age of humanity, from Adam to Noah, was, suggests the author of the *De Genesi,* like a human infancy, when men first began to enjoy the "light of the first day"; but as the memories of infancy are obliterated in the "deluge" of human growth, so was the first biblical age of humanity drowned away in Noah's Flood. The second age, which lasted from Noah to Abraham, might be likened to the second day of Creation, when God created the firmament: for Noah's ark was like a firmament separating the waters it floated upon from the waters which poured down. And as our childhood is never wiped from our memory, so was the second age of humanity not wiped out by a deluge. The third age of humanity, from Abraham to David, like the third day of Creation, witnessed the separation of the waters from the dry land; for it was during this period that the "dry land" of Abraham and his people, ever thirsting for the "rain" of divine law, was set apart from the sea of Gentile nations. And as in the life of man it is characteristic of adolescence to be a period of seed-making, which later enables men to sire offspring, so did the third age of humanity receive the "seed" of Scripture and the prophets and was thus enabled to engender the People of God. The fourth age, from David to the Babylonian captivity, like *iuventus* in the life of each man, is an "aetas aetatum," a culmination, which can naturally be likened to the fourth day of Creation, when God made the stars in the firmament of heaven. During the fifth age of man, from the Babylonian exile until Christ (an age of decline, *gravitas*), the Jews lived somewhat like the fishes and the birds of the fifth day of creation: like fishes they were scattered in the sea of alien nations; like birds they had no dwelling of their own. The sixth age of humanity, from the birth of Christ to the end of the world, can be compared to the sixth day of Creation, and to the old age of human life, for it witnesses the *senectus* of the Jewish nation and the birth of the "novus homo qui spiritualiter vivit." The seventh age of humanity is metahistorical; heralded by the second coming of Christ, it is to be followed by the "repose" of the seventh day, the eternal sabbath.[4]

For nearly a thousand years, most medieval chroniclers were to continue to look at universal history through Augustinian spectacles. Those ambitious enough to write a universal chronicle—and their name was legion—ultimately resorted to some variant of the Augustinian system in order to fit or serialize the events of biblical and secular history. Augustine's allegorical system, of course, allowed some room for play; but it was out of the question to presume that the basic model could ever be improved. So it was that in the early sixth century Fabius Claudius Fulgentius divided the "aetates mundi et hominis" into twenty-three periods corresponding to the twenty-three letters of the Latin alphabet; but though death prevented him from proceeding beyond the fourteenth age, he had written enough to make it clear to his reader that his system is merely an Augustinian loaf cut into finer slices. Isidore of Seville made use of the Augustinian system on several occasions, especially in his *Etymologiae* and *Differentiae*. Bede adopted the Augustinian analogy between the ages of humanity and the ages of man in his *Chronicon* of universal history from Adam to the year 729. From John Scotus Erigena in the ninth century, until Vincent de Beauvais and Bonaventure in the thirteenth, universal history continues to be serialized, categorized, and described in Augustinian terms. If one is patient enough to peruse these lengthy compendia, specula, or chronica, one concludes that Bonaventure is perhaps alone in giving proof of being able to digest the Augustinian system and express it in his own words.

From the fifth to the thirteenth century chroniclers of world history cast their accounts into a mold set either by Eusebius or by Augustine. In some cases, that of Augustine's disciple Orosius, for example, the Eusebian and Augustinian systems were both assimilated and transcended, to the enrichment of the work itself. More often than not, however, Augustine's sevenfold division provided a uniform and somewhat cramping mold, and chroniclers who fell victim to their excessive zeal for imitating the Church Fathers found themselves unable to think of history in any other way. By the end of the thirteenth century, interest in the Eusebian and Augustinian chronological systems and in universal chronicles in general began to decline. Chroniclers of the fourteenth and fifteenth centuries, writing mostly in the vernacular, were far more interested than their predecessors in focusing their vision on the particular history of the kingdom or duchy in which they lived and upon the princes who, more often than not, were their patrons. The reasons for this change of focus were both historical and philosophical. The Hundred Years' War between England and France (1337–1455) coincided within the main European universities with the so-called nominalist crisis. Philosophers like William of Ockham appeared less confident than their realist predecessors in the power of reason to encompass any apprehension of singulars within a universal concept, to connect any of the phenomena of history or life with one another, or to endow the myriad singulars of reality with any unifying nexus—whether Platonic essence or Providential mind. The results of this crisis were as disquieting for chroniclers as they were for poets, princes, and philosophers. With the start of the fourteenth century, historical writing, on the whole, began to concentrate its attention upon the present rather than the past, upon singulars rather than universals, upon the day-to-day events of kingdoms and empires rather than the history of salvation. European chroniclers set about measuring history in months, years, and days rather than with biblical, physiological, or geometric systems of chronology.[5]

The decline of the universal chronicle tradition in the fourteenth century coincides with the rise of a vernacular historiographical tradition and of a generally persistent attachment by the chroniclers themselves to well-circumscribed areas of space and time. Curiously enough the waning of chronicle writing with universal or ecumenical scope is roughly coeval with a crisis of deepening doubt, among philosophical figures, as to whether logical universals are anything save intra-mental figments. As a nominalist of the latter half of the fourteenth century might have found universals far too shaky for the edification of any rational system of philosophy, so do fourteenth- and fifteenth-century chroniclers seem to consider notions such as "Church," "Empire," or

"History of Salvation" as categories far too broad to be handled comfortably. Then too, historiographical particularism, whose scope is a specific city, kingdom, abbey, or duchy, appears at a time when princes themselves, the immense crusading effort of the twelfth and thirteenth centuries now past, seem no longer to think of Christendom as a universal category that transcends their own interests; and though the change of spirit just described is apparent around the time of Joinville's chronicle (ca. 1300), one detects warning signs of an inchoate fragmentation of Europe into rival polities and of a consequent particularization of European chronicle writing as far back as Villehardouin's account of the Franco-Venetian conquest of Constantinople a century earlier.

French historiography between 1200 and 1500 is largely a particularistic enterprise; but some of the chroniclers of the late medieval period were able to substitute for chronological systems which they innocently or explicitly disregarded their own structures of vision, perception, and thought. Each of them projected the light of his narrative on a limited circle of events, without endeavoring to interpret them according to any preordained system. Theirs was a private, sometimes solipsistic perception of historical reality, which offered the advantage of being unobstructed by the screen of erudition or previous historiographical tradition.

Before proceeding to separate examinations of seven Old French chronicles, it might be well to relate them to their times and to summarize the major events about which they revolve.

The Chroniclers and Their Context

The Fourth Crusade (1202–1204) widened the schism between the Roman papacy and the patriarchate of Constantinople and gave it an almost definitive stamp. Unlike the first three crusades, it was an entirely feudal affair. When Pope Innocent III sent his famous letter to King Richard I to express his indignation against those princes who were "wasting their time in pleasure and quarrel," none of them answered his call. Philip II Augustus of France had accompanied Richard I of England to the Holy Land in 1190, but during the quarter century separating his return (1191) from the battle of Bouvines (1214), Philip was engaged in almost perpetual warfare. His military campaigns against Richard I and his brother, John Lackland, in Normandy, Maine, Brittany, Touraine, Poitou, Anjou, and Aquitaine did not permit him to take the cross. John Lackland of England had just ascended the throne and was absorbed in civil strife with the barons. In Germany a struggle for the throne opposed Otto of Brunswick and Philip of Swabia, so that neither of them could leave the country. Alone among the sovereigns the king of Hungary took the cross. Nor was the crusade directed by Pope Innocent III. The crusade was led by an oligarchy of barons whose names and acts are known to us principally by way of Villehardouin's chronicle: Boniface de Montferrat, Baldwin and Henry of Flanders, Louis de Blois, Hugues de Saint-Pol, and Enrico Dandolo, the Venetian doge.[6]

The reasons that impelled the French barons to swear to take the cross were much like those that had given impetus to previous crusades: the barons were devout, brutal, fond of travel, adventure, and gain, sensitive to the plight of the holy places and the lure of gold, and aware of the necessity to do penance and gain indulgences in order to save their souls. Like the "conquistadores" of a later age, they sailed for a variety of reasons, not all of which were praiseworthy or mutually consistent.

The Fourth Crusade was the first to be decided upon in a courtly setting. At a tournament held at Ecri-sur-Aisne, November 28, 1199, the barons of Champagne swore to take the cross for the defense and recovery of the holy sepulchre. The barons of Picardy and Flanders soon followed this example.[7] The preacher whose eloquence set the crusade under way, Fulk of Neuilly, was cut of the same cloth as Peter the Hermit and Saint Bernard. "He often preached," said a contemporary chronicler, "on a public place in Paris called Champeaux. There the usurers, the prostitutes, the great sinners, taking off their clothes, . . . would fall at his feet and confess their sins. Sick people were often brought to him. The crowd would run after him, tear his cassock so as to share the shreds among themselves. In vain he would try to wave off the most impatient of them with his stick; he could not save his clothes from the pious avidity of the spectators."[8] When the curé of Neuilly set about collecting alms for the support of indigent crusaders in Syria, the enthusiasm of the crowds is said to have diminished somewhat. But there is no doubt—Villehardouin attests to this in the opening chapter of his chronicle—that the vows taken at the tournament of Ecri were an immediate result of the extraordinary success of Fulk's preaching throughout the Ile de France and of the "many miracles that God worked for him."

The barons at Ecri felt that the time was ripe. Count Thibaut of Champagne, who was their first choice to lead the expedition, died in 1201, before it could get under way. Upon the recommendation of Philip Augustus, Boniface of Montferrat was named to replace Thibaut. In keeping with a tradition established in previous crusades, most of the crusading knights wished to land in Syria and to attack Jerusalem from the north. The barons were of a different mind: this time Islam was to be attacked from the south, by way of Egypt. The argument seemed sound enough. The Christian princes in Syria, like fastidious colonial governors, had been out of touch with events in Europe and would surely look askance at the arrival of newcomers into kingdoms in which they felt well established. Egypt was an excellent stepping-stone to Palestine and to the entire Eastern Mediterranean basin. It was agreed by a majority of the barons at Ecri that Villehardouin and five other envoys should travel to Venice in order to conclude an agreement with the doge for the transportation of troops to Egypt.[9]

Soon the interests of the members of the coalition began to diverge. Many of the French knights who opposed the baronial plan to attack Palestine by way of Egypt decided, according to Villehardouin's obsessive phrase, to "sail from other ports." The Venetians, for their part, refused to transport any crusaders until the sum that had been agreed upon in their treaty with the barons had been paid in full. And when the barons discovered that they were unable to muster a sufficient number of troops to pay the full price of transport, they felt compelled to accept Doge Dandolo's offer to help the Venetians conquer the Dalmatian city of Zara, which had recently seceded from the Venetian empire in order to accept the protection of the king of Hungary.

The Franco-Venetian fleet left Venice in October 1202 and arrived within view of the walls of Zara in early November. The crusaders disregarded Pope Innocent III's order not to attack this Christian city and his threat to excommunicate the entire crusading army if they did. Nor were they deterred by the crucifixes that were affixed to the walls of Zara by its inhabitants. On November 24, 1202, the crusaders stormed the walls of Zara and took the city. Two months later, after camping all winter in Zara, the crusading force left for Corfu. Before leaving they burned the city to the ground.

The intricate events that follow are perhaps best summarized by Vasiliev:

> During the siege and surrender of Zara a new personality makes his appearance in the history of the Fourth Crusade—the Byzantine prince Alexius Angelus, son of the dethroned and blinded Isaac. Alexius had escaped from prison and fled to the West in order to obtain help for restoring the throne to his unfortunate father. After a fruitless meeting with the pope in Rome, the prince went to the north, to Germany, to his brother-in-law Philip of Swabia, who had married Irene, Alexius' sister and Isaac's daughter. Irene begged her husband to help her brother, who, "without shelter and fatherland, was traveling like the

floating stars and had nothing with him but his own body." Philip, who was at that time absorbed in his struggle with Otto of Brunswick, was unable to support Alexius effectively, but he sent an embassy to Zara begging Venice and the crusaders to help Isaac and his son by restoring them to the Byzantine throne. For that aid Alexius promised to subordinate Byzantium to Rome as far as religion was concerned, to pay a large amount of money, and, after restoring his father to the throne, to take a personal part in the crusade.[10]

Thus the direction of the crusade was irrevocably changed. Boniface de Montferrat was favorable to Alexius' request. As for the doge, Enrico Dandolo, now past eighty but as energetic and ambitious as ever, this was a long-awaited chance. "A legend relates that about thirty years before, Dandolo, during his stay in Constantinople as a hostage, had been treacherously blinded by the Greeks by means of a concave mirror which strongly reflected the rays of the sun; this circumstance was the cause of Dandolo's deep hatred of Byzantium."[11]

In April 1203 the Franco-Venetian fleet, headed by Dandolo, Boniface de Montferrat, and Prince Alexius, sailed from Corfu. In June, it entered the sea of Marmara, within sight of the walls of Constantinople. The city was besieged and taken in July. Isaac, Prince Alexius' imprisoned father, was released. In August, Prince Alexius was crowned Emperor Alexius IV of Constantinople and ruled as coregent with his father, Isaac II.

Between August 1203 and April 1204, relations between the Greeks and the crusaders, which had been so cordial during the period of euphoria that preceded and followed the liberation of the city, grew cool at first, then hostile. Alexius could not immediately honor the commitment he had made at Zara to pay the crusaders a large sum of money and accompany them to Egypt with an army of ten thousand men. He demanded that the crusading army cease its encampment in Constantinople and withdraw to the suburbs of the city, across the Golden Horn. Meanwhile, within the city, traditionally peaceful relations between Greek and Latin residents became strained. Greek residents grew resentful of the rule of the coregents, whom they accused of having capitulated to the crusaders. "An insurrection burst out. The son-in-law of Emperor Alexius III, the ambitious Alexius Ducas Mourtzouphlos, was proclaimed emperor at the beginning of 1204, Isaac II and Alexius IV were deposed. Isaac died very soon in prison; and Alexius IV, by order of Mourtzouphlos, was strangled."[12]

After the murder of Alexius IV, the crusaders considered themselves freed of any former promises to Constantinople. In April they sailed across the Golden Horn, stormed the walls of the city, and took it a second time. Baldwin of Flanders was proclaimed Latin Emperor of the East. Within four years the conquered territory included Thrace, parts of Macedonia, and the Peloponnesus (Morea). "The conquered territory was divided by the Emperor into a great number of larger or smaller fiefs, for the possession of which the Western knights were obliged to take vassal oath to the Latin Emperor of Constantinople."[13]

Such was the chain of events forged by the agreement made with Prince Alexius Angelus at Zara. Was the conquest of Constantinople premeditated? Was it an accident? Had Venice, as some historians pretend, made a secret agreement with the sultan of Egypt even before its treaty with the crusaders? Did Boniface de Montferrat consult with King Philip of Swabia before the departure of the fleet from Venice and were arrangements for the deviation of the crusade known to some of the barons beforehand? "Until about 1860," remarks Vasiliev, "no dispute on that problem had existed, because all historians had depended mainly on the statements of the chief western source of the Fourth Crusade and a participant in it, the French historian Geoffroy de Villehardouin. In his exposition the events of the crusade progressed simply and accidentally: not having vessels, the crusaders hired them at Venice and therefore assembled there; after having hired the vessels they could not pay the Republic of Saint Mark the full amount fixed and were forced to support the Venetians in their strife with Zara; then followed the coming of the prince Alexius, who inclined the crusaders against Byzantium. Thus, there was no question of any treason of Venice nor of any complicated intrigue."[14]

The "theory of premeditation" was put forward for the first time in 1861 by the French scholar, Mas-Latrie. It was adopted by Count de Riant in 1875 and has found various proponents during the past century. In recent years, especially since Edmond Faral's exhaustive article on the problem of Villehardouin's sincerity, the premeditation theory, though it may continue to appeal to those who enjoy reading between the lines of history, has fallen into relative disfavor. The full details of the Fourth Crusade will perhaps never be known.

Sire Jean de Joinville's lifetime (1225–1317) spanned the reigns of Louis IX (1226–70), Philip III (1270–85), Philip the Fair (1286–1314), and Louis X (1315–16). Parts of his chronicle (Chapter 17, for example) refer to events that took place during the reign of Philip Augustus (1181–1214). Although Joinville's *Life of Saint Louis* purports to concentrate on the events of one reign, the book was begun during the reign of Philip III and commissioned by Jeanne of Navarre, the wife of Philip the Fair, around 1298 or so. By the time Joinville wrote his dedicatory opening paragraph in 1309, the queen had been dead for four years.

As one examines the genesis of Joinville's work and the chronology of its evolution, one is impressed both by the author's refusal to be pressed for time and by the curiously tepid tone of the book when it does appear. The *Life of Saint Louis* is written in a key of reticence. Joinville had much to be reticent about. He might have had grave reservations as to the powerful influence on Saint Louis of the queen mother, Blanche of Castille, not only during her regency (1226–34), but during the first two decades of her son's reign. Like his contemporary, the commoner-poet Rutebeuf, Joinville can only have questioned Saint Louis's misguided confidence in the ability of crusading expeditions to solve Mediterranean political problems; his gullibility and excessive largesse toward some of the mendicant orders of his time; and his laxness in bringing to heel his ambitious, gaming brother, Duke Charles of Anjou, whose conquest of the kingdom of Sicily was to entangle his Capetian and Valois descendants in Italian affairs for the next three centuries. Like Rutebeuf, Joinville might have complained that

> Sus cest siècle qu'adès empire
> Ou refroidier voi charité;
> Ausi s'en vont sans avoir mire
> La ou li deables les tire,
> Qui Dieu en a desherité.[15]

(In this world which is now growing worse,/Wherein charity is growing cold,/Those whom God has disinherited/Are going wherever the devil leads them,/And they don't care.)

It was perhaps as a member of the feudal nobility that Joinville had the greatest cause for reticence. The most dramatic feature of the history of France between the official accession of Louis IX (1234) and that of the first Valois, Philip VI (1328), is the progressive centralization of monarchical institutions in France.[16] Such a centralization could only be achieved at the expense of feudal privilege. Despite his admiration for the king, Joinville must have been an unwilling and occasionally grumbling witness of the decline of those ancient privileges to which he held dearly. The *Life of Saint Louis* betrays his attachment to the feudal, chivalric code which to his mind takes clear precedence over written law or monarchical privilege.

King Louis IX centered his entire domestic and external policy about the concept of a strong monarchical authority. In this regard he con-

solidated a structure whose foundations had been laid by his grandfather, Philip Augustus. In the name of national and monarchical interest, Louis IX did commit a number of political blunders which Joinville
was not the first to take note of. The king did not officially encourage
Charles of Anjou's hostility to Emperor Frederick II's descendents (with
whom Joinville had family ties); nor did he give his blessing to his
brother's ill-advised expedition to Sicily. But he did nothing to prevent
them. For his failure he was berated by feudal nobility and commoners
alike. In a curious allegorical satire written around 1270, Rutebeuf takes
"Noble the Lion" (King Louis IX) to task for allowing the kingdom to
fall into the hands of a perverted fox (Renart le Bestornier) who is
about to plunge the whole kingdom into war:

> Renars porra mouvoir tel guerre
> Dont mout bien se porroit souferre
>   La regions.
> Me sires Nobles li lyons
> Cuide que sa sauvations
>   De Renart viegne.[17]

(Renart may start a war that will bring/Great suffering to the kingdom.
/But Sir Noble the Lion thinks that his/Salvation comes from Renart.)

King Louis's ill-timed and ill-fated crusade to Tunis, undertaken when,
as Joinville put it, "the kingdom was at peace within and without," was
largely a product of the king's misappraisal of the complex balance of
forces between Christians and Moslems in the Mediterranean. When the
king took the cross for the second time in 1267, he was convinced that
the "roi de Thunes" (the sultan of Tunis) was about to convert to
Christianity. It had been a lifelong dream with King Louis to restore the
Christian faith to North Africa, where it had flourished at the time of
the Church Fathers. But, as he had underestimated the strength of the
Mongols in Eastern Europe in 1240, and the fierce determination of the
Saracens at Mansourah, so did he misjudge the dangers and complexi-
ties of a landing at Tunis in 1270.

Within the kingdom itself, Joinville found more immediate cause for
dissatisfaction. Louis IX had accelerated, whenever he did not inaugu-
rate, the whittling down of feudal privileges to which the nobility was
particularly attached: the right to bear arms in tournaments, the right
to engage in private wars, the right to use ancient judicial procedures
such as the feudal judiciary duel. But King Louis replaced the duel by
an investigational procedure, based on Canon law. In January 1258, he
outlawed all private wars in the lands of the royal domain. In instituting

"les avoueries," he gave commoners the right to waive or withdraw from feudal jurisdiction by "avowing" that they were "king's men." The king's sergeants often broke into feudal domains whenever a "royal pretext" seemed to justify their doing so. A contemporary balladeer complained that a France wherein such abuses are rife cannot be called "douce" but "acuvertie" (degenerate).[18]

The *Life of Saint Louis* could appear to some readers like a treatise *de regimine principum,* wherein a former king's steward presents Louis's descendants with an idealized, though human picture of their forebear, in the hope that they will take inspiration from his sanctity, wisdom, and justice. But seen in another light it also reads like a delicate expression of nostalgia, written by a conservative feudal lord, for the days when *preudomie* (chivalric bravery) was an ideal to which even kings paid homage.

Froissart's lifetime (ca. 1337–after 1400) coincided, roughly, with the reigns of Philip VI (1328–50), John the Good (1350–64), Charles V (1364–80), and Charles VI (1380–1422). During Froissart's century, particularly the latter half, historical reality began to be considered as a horizontal rather than a vertical structure. The reasons for this flattening of historical vision are both complex and interrelated. Ockham's razor had dealt scholastic metaphysics a deadly cut.[19] No longer could the philosophic house of intellect be featured as a structure as immovable as the Gothic arch, its bases firmly set on the pillars of sense experience, its centripetal ribs joining together at the vault-key of "real universals," which crown the structure and gave it both unity and cohesion. Real knowledge now seems reduced to what the mind can muster through sense perception. Universal essences begin to appear as insubstantial as the vault of heaven, providing an airy cover and an illusory shelter. Things seem to be falling apart; their nexus of cohesion is not a principle inscribed in things themselves but a figment produced by the mind of the beholders. Reality now seems an impressive but disjunctive agglomeration of ruins on a flat, wasted earth.

The impact of these new ideas was felt in every sphere of fourteenth-century life. In the life and literature of the twelfth and thirteenth centuries, the world was felt to have a unity both symbolic and real. Writers and artists were convinced that there existed a structural bond between a *figura* and its *sensus,* between sense appearance and the substance of things unseen. One need only reflect upon the "reality" of a concept like *preudomie* to Joinville's mind. So all-englobing is that general category

that it appears more important than any of the particulars it incorpo-
rates, including Saint Louis himself. In the thirteenth-century chronicle
a universal concept, a moral ideal, are somehow superior, nobler, than
any of the singular instances, cases, or examples which they represent.
For any of Joinville's scholastic contemporaries, essence takes both logical and ontological precedence over existence. One ask "quid sit" of a
thing before asking "an sit." The moral life is an area governed by universal principles, each of which serves as a guide in the "inferior" world
of particular action.

But Ockham's ideas now underscored the essentially problematic
character of man's rapport with reality. The world has begun to appear
an agglomeration of colorful but disconnected and hazy images. The
backdrop of history seems deceitful, covered as it is with false perspec-
tives and optical illusions. Lying is no longer considered a scandalous
betrayal of reality, but simply one mistake among many others. In the
fourteenth century, the aristocratic ideal cannot be taken as seriously
as it was at the time of Villehardouin and Joinville. The bourgeois, the
people, have lost faith in the aristocracy, which has lost faith in itself.
No longer can an aristocrat think of himself as fulfilling a divinely ordained mission in a universe where he knows his place. The aristocracy
itself has lost its sense of being divinely commissioned, its sense of being
chivalric; having lost its metaphysical justification, it must now play the
game of chivalry. And to play that game, as Froissart's chronicle
shows, the aristocracy needs plenty of space, plenty of décor, and plenty
of money.[20]

The evolution of aristocratic attitudes in fourteenth-century France
was very much a product of successive historical catastrophes: the defeats of Crécy (1346), Poitiers (1356), and Agincourt (1415) each
decimated French chivalry and exhausted it. The decline of the aristocracy in France was accompanied by a converse awakening of the third
estate. History seems to have democratized the social structures quite
as much as Ockham had democratized logic. In both realms particulars
were felt to have an importance of their own. The resentment of the
common people toward an increasingly dissolute aristocracy was perhaps best described by a major chronicler of the reign of King John the
Good. Around the time of the battle of Poitiers, Jean de Venette complained that

> the luxury and dissoluteness of many of the nobles and the knights
> became still more deeply rooted. I have described above the far too
> brief and scanty garments which they had already adopted. Now they
> began to disfigure themselves in a still more extravagant way. They

wore pearls on their hoods or on their gilded and silver girdles and elaborately adorned themselves from head to foot with gems and precious stones. So assiduously did all men, from the least to the greatest, cover themselves with these luxuries that pearls and other precious stones were sold for high prices and could hardly be found at all in Paris. . . . Men also began to wear the plumes of birds fastened on their hats. By night they devoted themselves immoderately to the pleasures of the flesh or to games of dice; by day, to ball or tennis. Wherefore the common people had reason to lament, and did lament greatly, that the taxes levied on them for the war were uselessly spent on such sport and converted to such uses.[21]

Venette also ruefully mentions the aristocratic habit of deriding peasants and simple folk by calling them Jacques Bonhomme. "But woe is me! many who had derided peasants with this name were later made mental sport of by them. For many nobles, as shall be told, perished miserably at the hands of peasants."

At Poitiers, King John was captured by the Black Prince, taken to London, and held for a large ransom. Charles, duke of Normandy, John's eldest son, returned to Paris, where he was at first well received. He was named regent, and the French kingdom was governed by a coalition of representatives from the clergy, the nobility, and the common people.

Thus discord arose, and all three estates abandoned the task they had begun. From that time on all went ill with the kingdom, and the state was undone. Thieves and robbers rose up everywhere in the land. The nobles despised and hated all others and took no thought for the mutual usefulness and profit of lords and men. They subjected and despoiled the peasants and the men of the villages. In no wise did they defend their country from its enemies. Rather did they trample it underfoot, robbing and pillaging the peasants' goods. The regent, it appeared clearly, gave no thought to their plight. At that time the country and whole land of France began to put on confusion and mourning like a garment, because it had no defender or guardian.[22]

By the middle of the fourteenth century, history thus appeared a "horizontal" rather than a "vertical" construct. Social and political structures were leveled. As one considers the most poignant moments of Froissart's chronicle one notices that the aristocracy must share the stage with burghers, commoners, and peasants. The burghers of Calais, though they are forced to surrender the keys of their city to King Edward III, reveal a courage and a determination which in former days would have been shown by the aristocracy alone. By 1346 the moral

vitality of the French political body is to be found not in its head—
King Philip VI is helpless in the face of this disaster—but in its members. After the defeat at Poitiers, it is a Parisian merchant, Etienne Marcel, who heads the opposition of the Parisian burghers to the arbitrary
taxation of the commoners. Despite Froissart's instinctive mistrust of
peasant mobs, his account of the uprising and repression of the Jacquerie
and of the Wat Tyler rebellion depicts a peasantry in both England and
France that is growing progressively conscious of age-old class oppres-
sion. And the restoration of order and respect for the monarchy throughout the French kingdom during the decade 1370–80 is the work of an
obscure figure of provincial stock, Bertrand Du Guesclin, a commoner
and peasant, who describes himself as "a poor man, of base extraction."

The leveling spirit of the century seems to have affected the chroniclers themselves. Historical writing, once the prerogative of monks and
aristocrats, was now being written by clerics, courtesans, and burghers.
Villehardouin's French chronicle in the early thirteenth century had
been the first example of its kind to be written in the vernacular. Joinville's *Life of Saint Louis* is one the first medieval biographies to be
written in French. But in Froissart's time, most chronicles were being
written in French prose. The departure of historiography from its sacred
references was dramatized by its symbolic departure from Latin, the
language of sacrament. History, like other literary genres (lyric poetry,
for example), was slowly imbued with a naturalistic spirit. The life of
man was no longer felt to be a participation in either a divine mystery,
a divine mission, or a universal ideal. The sacred tone that had so characterized the crusade chronicles of the twelfth and thirteenth centuries,
the quasi-religious attachment of a Villehardouin or a Joinville to their
mission or their class, gave way to a spirit of levity or raillery, which
revealed a deep-rooted pessimism. "On the whole," says Huizinga of
the late fourteenth and early fifteenth centuries, "civilization became
more serious."[23]

Paradoxically enough, because it is considered a serious but not a
sacred phenomenon, history around Froissart's time begins to be viewed
as a linear succession of fascinating images. Since reality is essentially
sense experience, history is basically a roll, a register (Froissart's word
for describing the basic historiographical act is *enregistrer*). Sense reality being no longer considered the *figura* that refers to a concealed
sensus, images are considered for themselves, all the more fascinating
because they are passing and colorful, and because the hidden sense
they conceal has grown increasingly obscure. Nature, in Froissart's time,
is no longer a mirror of the divine presence. To the historian's eye, ever
curious for striking images and positive sensations, reality has lost its

metaphysical, sacred character. The interstices of things reveal not hidden essences but the void and curious workings of Chance.[24] There is no hidden message between the lines of Froissart's chronicle. If the chronicler of Froissart's time cannot create his own essences, he must despair of attaining them with his mind.

In the final act of Shakespeare's *Henry V,* Duke Philip of Burgundy sketches a picture of the French kingdom around the end of the reign of King Charles VI. The defeat at Agincourt has plunged the Valois monarchy into its deepest agony since the capture of King John the Good at Poitiers three quarters of a century before. The Treaty of Troyes (1420) is about to arrange the marriage of King Henry V to Catherine of France, the eldest daughter of the French king. According to the terms of the treaty, Henry V, now the only "legitimate" son of the Crown of France, is to allow his French "father" to retain "the crown and royal dignity of France with all its revenues." Henry, on the other hand, is to acquire "the power to govern and order the public weal." Henry is to be called not "King of France" but "Heir to the King of France," but he is to rule even those territories over which the king of France has nominal control. Charles VI, who now alternates constantly between madness and despondency, wants peace, having no other alternative. Shakespeare's duke of Burgundy is a rather sanguine version of the historical model. His tone is mellifluous; his air is generally paternalistic. What impediment is there, he cries, "that the naked, poor, and mangled Peace/ . . . should not in this best garden of the world/Our fertile France, put up her lovely visage?"

> And as our vineyards, fallows, meads and hedges,
> Defective in their natures, grow to wildness,
> Even so our houses and ourselves and children
> Have lost, or do not learn for want of time,
> The sciences that should become our country;
> But grow like savages—as soldiers will
> That nothing do but meditate on blood,—
> To swearing and stern looks, defused attire
> And every thing that seems unnatural.
> Which to reduce into our former favour
> You are assembled: and my speech entreats
> That I may know the let, why gentle Peace
> Should not expel these inconveniences
> And bless us with her former qualities.
>   [*Henry V.* V. 1]

Duke Philip had every reason to desire peace. Ever since the death of Charles V, in 1380, the Burgundian star had waxed as the French had waned. Every round of warfare between France and England had left Burgundian territory intact. During the reign of Charles VI (1380–1422), the Burgundian duchy had become the most powerful in Europe and the most intelligently governed. Never does it engage in entangling alliances, rarely in disastrous crusades. During the minority of Charles VI (1380–89), while the duke of Anjou is away in Sicily attempting to recover the kingdom of Sicily from Aragon, it is Duke Philip the Hardy of Burgundy who to all purposes runs the French kingdom, wines and dines the young king in his duchy, woos the Council of Regents into arranging a marriage between Charles VI and Isabella of Bavaria (1385), and abstains from the crusading expedition against the Turks in the Balkans, which ends disastrously with the slaughter of the French army at Nicopolis (1396). By the year 1400, the Burgundian duchy is the most solidly established in Europe. While Richard II is deposed (1399) and Charles VI fights to retain his sanity after a series of mental breakdowns, Burgundy's destinies are presided over by two politically astute princes, Philip the Hardy (1393–1404) and John the Fearless (1404–19).

"All things considered," Philippe de Commynes was to write of fifteenth-century politics, "it seems to me that God has created neither man nor beast in this world without establishing some counterpart to oppose him, in order to keep him in humility and fear."[25] In 1400, the counterpart to Burgundy was the house of Orléans. Duke Philip the Hardy's death in 1404—he had ruled since 1393—did not put an end to the rivalry between Armagnacs (the Orléans faction) and Burgundians. He was succeeded by his son, Duke John the Fearless. Between 1404 and 1407, hostility between the Armagnacs and the Burgundians grew to such a point that civil war seemed inevitable. Louis of Orléans's coat of arms bore the motto, "Je l'ennuie" ("I annoy him"). The duke of Burgundy's countered with an even more enterprising inscription in Flemish: "Ich oud" ("I have him"). On a November night in 1407, the duke of Orléans was stabbed and killed by six or eight masked assassins in the streets of Paris. Two days later Duke John the Fearless admitted that he had ordered the killing. Civil war between Armagnacs and Burgundians hung fire for several years. But neither duchy had enough money to wage war, and subsequent developments in England prevented it from ever taking place. King Henry IV died in 1413. Two years later, Henry V broke a thirty-five-year truce with France and landed a large army at Calais. In October 1415 he destroyed the French army at Agincourt, took several thousand prisoners, and massacred several thousand more. In 1420, he entered Rouen, after a siege that decimated the civilian population. In 1420, he dictated the Treaty of Troyes. The final act of this mad, absurd drama was as ironic as it was brief: within five months of the Treaty of Troyes, both the humiliated French king and his triumphant English "heir" were dead.

Louis of Orléans had been murdered by Burgundian assassins at the instigation of Duke John the Fearless of Burgundy. In July 1419 the duke of Burgundy in turn met a violent death at the hands of Armagnac assassins at Montereau, at the instigation of the dauphin, Charles. Burgundy then allied itself with England for the next two decades: on Christmas Day 1419 King Henry V and the young successor to Burgundy, Duke Philip the Good, signed a treaty of military alliance. One of the sword blows that killed John the Fearless had pierced his skull. A century after the assassination, a Chartreux monk showed King Francis I the hole in the skull of the murdered Burgundian prince and remarked: "Sire, that is the hole through which the English came into France."

The history of France and Burgundy during the reigns of King Charles VII (1422–61) and Duke Philip the Good (1419–67) is one of slow national revival on the one hand and of uninterrupted prosperity on the other. When King Charles VI died, in October 1422, his son Charles became king of Bourges. The prestige, power, and wealth of the French monarchy had never been so low. The English had taken Paris in 1419; they were to remain there until 1436. According to the Treaty of Troyes, all of France north of the Loire was to become the birthright of the English crown after the death of Charles VI. Between 1422 and 1430 an inert and secretive Charles VII hid in his closets at Bourges, while a few of his father's most faithful administrators tried to restore some semblance of monarchic administration at Bourges and Poitiers. In 1429, a young peasant girl from the eastern marches had ridden more than four hundred miles, from Vaucouleurs to Chinon, to convince the young king of France that he should ride to Rheims to be crowned. This Charles was finally persuaded to do; but when Joan of Arc was captured at Compiègne, in May 1430, after lifting the siege of Orléans, Charles made no effort to ransom or rescue her from her Burgundian captors or her English jailers.

At the time of Joan's capture, Normandy, the Ile de France, and Guyenne were still in English hands. After her death, the tide of war began to turn. The king's evil genius, La Trémoille, who had been so hostile to Joan, was dismissed in 1433. In 1435, Duke Philip of Burgundy broke his alliance with England, and death took the duke of Bedford, who was not only the greatest of the English captains, but the only public figure capable of averting an imminent civil war in England between the houses of Lancaster and York.

Charles VII, a prematurely old and fear-ridden king at twenty, became a confident administrator in middle age. In 1445, he created a permanent army of regular, paid soldiers and, in 1448, an elite guard of tax-exempt archers, the *franci-sagittarii*. In 1449, taking advantage of the civil war raging in England, he struck at Normandy, which had been an English fief since the victory of Agincourt. Within two years he had reconquered Rouen, Harfleur, and Honfleur. In 1451, he invaded the last English stronghold in France, the province of Guyenne, which had been an English possession since the time of Henry II Plantagenet. The capture of Bordeaux in 1455 brought to a close three centuries of warfare over the possession of Guyenne. At the time of Charles's death, in 1461, the French monarchy had regained a prestige which it had not held since the death of Charles V.

The "French revival" had not failed to impress Christendom; but, after a century of fighting, France remained a poor cousin to Burgundy, which continued to cast an ominous shadow over the throne. France had been bled white by the war. At the time of the accession of Louis XI (1461), many parts of the French kingdom lay desolate and waste, despite Charles VII's efforts to reconstruct French agriculture, artisanship, and industry, and despite the proverbial industriousness of the French character, which the Burgundian chronicler Georges Chastellain described as "non paresseux, ne tardif." On his way to Paris after the death of his father, the young Louis XI complained that he had found nothing but ruins, sterile and uncultivated fields, poor and emaciated men and women.[26] Sir John Fortescue, after a trip through France around 1465, wrote in his *Governance of England* that "they live in extreme misery; yet they inhabit the most fertile kingdom on earth."[27] The duke of Burgundy's description of "this best garden of the world," waste and desolate at the time of the Treaty of Troyes, still held true at the time of the coronation of Louis XI:

> Alas, she [Peace] hath from France too long been chased,
> And all her husbandry doth lie on heaps,
> Corrupting in its own fertility.
> Her vine, the merry cheerer of the heart,
> Unpruned dies; her hedges even-pleached,
> Like prisoners wildly overgrown with hair,

Put forth disordered twigs; her fallow leas
The darnel, hemlock and rank fumitory,
Doth root upon, while that the coulter rusts
That should deracinate such savagery;
The even mead, that erst brought sweetly forth
The freckled cowslip, burnet and green clover,
Wanting the scythe, all uncorrected, rank,
Conceives by idleness and nothing teems
But hateful docks, rough thistles, kecksies, burs
Losing both beauty and utility.

[*Henry V*. V. 1]

During the same period, the power and wealth of Burgundy had continued to grow. When Duke Philip the Good attended the coronation of his nephew, Louis XI, the splendor of his dress and the impressiveness of his train outshone the king's. In his official acts he called himself "duke of Burgundy, of Lothier, of Brabant and of Limburg, count of Flanders, of Artois, and of Burgundy, palatin of Hainaut, of Holland of Zeeland and of Namur, marquess of the Holy Empire, lord of Frisia, of Salins, and of Malines." By mid-century he had almost doubled his patrimony: he had bought the county of Namur and the duchy of Luxemburg; he had inherited the duchies of Brabant and of Limburg; he had dispossessed Jacqueline of Hainaut of Holland, Zeeland, and Frisia. During his alliance with the duke of Bedford he had carved out parts of the domains of Charles VII, especially the Somme towns of Amiens, Péronne, and Saint-Quentin. He had secretly encouraged the young dauphin, Louis, to conspire against his father. He had granted him asylum in Flanders in 1456. At that time, King Charles VII had uttered a phrase which, twenty years later, would carry a ring of prophecy: "My cousin of Burgundy is feeding the fox that will eat his chickens."[28]

Such was the spectacle that Georges Chastellain, and later Olivier de La Marche, were to mirror in their courtly chronicles. Both had risen slowly through the ranks of service as squires, cup-bearers, and chamberlains. The role of historiographer was considered but one, however prestigious, of the several avenues of service. The Burgundian dukes had never made it their policy to subsidize literary merit for its own sake; they believed literature to be one of the ways of furthering the political interests of Burgundy. It was hard for a chronicler whose pension and presence at court were a constant reminder of his condition of protégé not to accept the duty to flatter that such a condition entailed. Burgundian literature, especially that of the reign of Duke Philip, was overtly official and sycophantic. It was written specifically for the glorification of a dynasty. "The education of a prince," asserted Duke Philip, "is the source of a nation's happiness." He considered historical books as instruments whereby the condition of his subjects might be bettered. Libraries, he thought, should contain national annals and other historical documents enabling the people to learn about the origins of laws and customs, about religions, and about matters political, social, religious, and economic.

The Burgundian court promised its historiographers security and the luxuries of life, but compressed their vision within the narrowest limits. Some historiographers seemed to conform—overtly, at least—to the dukes' expectations. Others could never have done so. In this regard, the defection of Philippe de Commynes from the service of the Burgundian dukes, in 1472, is symbolic. Although he never held the rank of Burgundian historiographer, Commynes might well have become one had he remained with Duke Charles the Bold. His decision to "defect" to Louis XI, after eight years of service with Charles (who succeeded Philip the Good as duke of Burgundy after Philip's death in 1467) was both coldly practical and prophetic: he realized that, within less than a generation, feudal particularism would give way to national unity. Viewed from a historiographical perspective, Commynes's *Memoirs,* coming as they do at the end of the fifteenth century, illustrate history in a new key, the particularist chronicle speaking a universal language.

The triumph of the monarchical idea in France during the latter half of the fifteenth century seems to coincide with a renewal of confidence among chroniclers in universal ideas. Begun during the reign of Charles VII, this new confidence is evident throughout Thomas Basin's chronicles, especially in his repeated claim that history is an intelligible enterprise; it reaches its culmination in the *Memoirs* of Commynes who, though he is writing a chronicle whose scope is limited in time, transmits maxims of political and moral wisdom that apply to all humanity.

Bishop Thomas Basin has much in common with his contemporaries, Chastellain, La Marche, and Commynes. Like the Burgundian historiographers, he is frequently pompous, long-winded, and one-sided. He has more in common with Commynes, however, than with any other chronicler of the fifteenth century. Like the lord of Argenton, he was not simply a narrator of facts, however colorful; he wished historical writing to be a school that might serve as a moral lesson to subsequent generations. He referred to himself as a "Veridicus relator et historicus verax" (trustworthy chronicler and truthful historian), an epithet Commynes would not have scorned. Basin believed that history, no matter how biased or involved the historian, can teach a lesson; no matter how circumscribed the chronicle in time and space, no matter how private and passion-ridden the chronicler's experience, he can distill from it a universal message of rational and communicable experience.

Both Commynes and Basin use heavily conceptual rather than metaphorical language. The syntax of their sentences is clear, the logical connections between propositions clearly articulated. Their use of irony is widesepread, in Basin's case heavy-footed, almost savage. The wide use of this rhetorical tool almost precludes the use of metaphor; for irony and metaphor are, on the whole, mutually exclusive, the function of metaphor being to reveal the ambiguities of language, while that of irony to hide them. Metaphor is diffusive, while irony is divisive.

Both authors might be described as attempting to read their own wisdom into the events of their time, or better, to transform their own vision of life into a philosophy of history. For Basin, the ultimate reality is God as Idea; hence his tendency to consider the collective life of peoples, as his own, in conceptual, antithetical terms. Basin is perhaps the most cerebral of all the chroniclers. His characters are disincarnate to the point of seeming almost personifications of preconceived concepts: Charles VII is the symbol of the good king, Louis XI an almost melodramatically wolfish villain. Spheres, styles, and orders are often rigorously opposed. Things seen by the historian are distinguished sharply from rumors and wives' tales; rational certitude is implicitly set off from both superstition and religious faith; the sphere of supernatural grace seems to exclude the lower sphere of necessity; vulgar opinion is something different from aristocratic opinion; feudal opinions and privileges raise more passion and seem to contain a more inherent necessity than those of commoners and peasants.

Commynes the soldier, ambassador, and man of action, on the other hand, views his own life and that of nations in terms of energy: its source, its concentration, deterioration, and redistribution. Energy is first concentrated at a primeval source, then lost, then reconcentrated in different forms. The entire universe seems to function according to some secret equation. History has always been a matter of personal ups and downs; of a primeval energy which reaches a peak, then wanes; of empires, kingdoms, and duchies in a state of rise and decline; of constant rearrangements of personal and collective energies, the disintegration of one being both cause and necessary condition for the rise of another.

Why should Basin and Commynes, both of whom had every reason to write biased accounts, have arrived at least implicitly at what it is not exaggerated to call a cosmic view of history? What is there about the reigns of Charles VII and Louis XI that suddenly raised the writing of history to a level of sophistication that did not seem possible to writers like Villehardouin, Joinville, Froissart, or even the Burgundian chroniclers? The answer may be in part biographical. More than any of the previous chroniclers, Basin and Commynes suffered at the hands of history; both might have divided their lives into a first period of political and social favor and a second period of disfavor and exile. Moreover, Basin's training as a classical humanist, his obvious need to imitate Sallust and Suetonius in Ciceronian cadences, gave him a range of vision that was not possible to any of the previous chroniclers. Commynes's wide travels, wherein he was actively engaged in implementing King Louis XI's twofold art of "dividing so as to command," gave him the best possible training in the subtle distinctions of language and the refinements of logic.

But biographical insights like these do not in themselves explain why two historians should almost simultaneously experience the need to transform a private vision of the world into universal language; unless, that is, one assumes that by the second half of the fifteenth century chroniclers were acquiring a sense of mission that transcended personal or parochial ends. It is noteworthy, in this regard, that Commynes is the first of the French medieval chroniclers to give his chronicle a European dimension. Froissart's stage is wider than Commynes's, but he fails to produce a universal category which in Commynes's *Memoirs* becomes a usable and workable instrument of language: the idea of Europe as a political collectivity.[29] With Commynes, Europe is spoken of for the first time, in France at least, as a balance of forces. The material world is a world of change, and change cannot be effected without loss of energy. This realization helps explain Commynes's almost physical sense of insecurity and metaphysical anxiety.

The virtual disappearance of world chronicles and of a sacred view of history in late medieval Europe did not by any means entail the disappearance of chronicles with an implicit world-view. No matter how limited their scope and substance, no matter how biased or parochial the minds that produced them, chronicles of the fourteenth and fifteenth centuries continued to illustrate some of the several world-views held at the time. Chroniclers in France from Villehardouin to Commynes continued to be witnesses to those materials which the literary public held most significant; and in this regard they spoke for the sense of importance held at least by the most literate of their contemporaries. One of the larger questions raised by each of the following chapters considers the evolution of this very sense of importance: was it essentially a projection of external events, or merely a product of private idiosyncracy or prejudice? While attempting to understand a most elusive period in the history of medieval historiography, we shall also raise the central question whether human perception is not itself a creation of history.

2 VILLEHARDOUIN: HISTORY IN BLACK AND WHITE

VILLEHARDOUIN lived most of his life during the latter half of the twelfth century, but his *Conquest of Constantinople,* dictated in French from his castle in Thrace, belongs to the early thirteenth.[1] Born before 1150 at Valenciennes, about twenty miles from Troyes, Villehardouin came from one of the best-known aristocratic families of Champagne. The title of "Maréchal," which he bore from 1185 onwards, made him the grey eminence of Count Thibaud III of Champagne. When the count, along with several other French barons, annnounced at the tournament of Ecri in November 1199 that he was preparing a crusade *outremer,* it was only natural that Villehardouin should come along. Villehardouin was one of six delegates sent to Venice by the French barons in order to arrange with the doge, Enrico Dandolo, for the transportation of twenty thousand crusaders, with their horses and arms, to the Holy Land. The Fourth Crusade was in the making.

Villehardouin's activities during the entire expedition were as varied as they were essential. He was one of the barons who argued for the "necessity" of diverting the Franco-Venetian expedition to Constantinople in order to chase the usurper, Alexius Mourtzouphlos, from the Byzantine throne. When Mourtzouphlos, terrified by the presence of the fleet in the harbor of the city, abdicated and fled in June 1203, Villehardouin was delegated by the French army to obtain from the rightful emperor, Isaac II, a confirmation of the commitments that had been made to the crusaders by his son, the young Alexius Angelus. After the conquest and sack of Constantinople by the crusaders in April 1204, and the ensuing conquest of Thrace, Villehardouin almost single-handedly avoided a civil war between the two most powerful barons, Boniface de Montferrat and Baldwin of Flanders, and their factions over the question of the occupation of Thessalonica.

Villehardouin was both a distinguished negotiator and a courageous warrior. After the death of Matthieu de Montmorency, he became the leader of the Champagne faction of the French army, and (between 1205 and 1208) participated in several victorious campaigns in Thrace. In 1205 he was named "Maréchal de Champagne et de Roumaine." He died between 1212 and 1218. The exact time and place of his death are unknown.

Villehardouin's chronicle records the events he witnessed between the year 1198, when the hermit Fulk of Neuilly began preaching the Fourth Crusade, and the year 1207, when Boniface de Montferrat was killed by the Bulgars in Thrace. He does not seem to have divided his account into books or chapters, but it happens, quite naturally, to fall into two parts. In Part One (chapters 1–58 of Edmond Faral's edition) he relates the chain of events leading up to the conquest of Constantinople in April 1204: Fulk of Neuilly's predication throughout the Ile de France; Villehardouin's trip to Venice; his agreement with the doge over the matter of maritime transportation; the assembly of the barons and knights at Venice; the conquest of Zara; the arrival of the fleet before Constantinople; the first conquest of the city; the restoration of the young Alexius Angelus after the capitulation of Alexius Mourtzouphlos; the conspiracy of Mourtzouphlos; the second conquest and the sack of the city by the crusaders and the coronation of Baldwin of Flanders as Latin emperor of Constantinople. The second part of the narrative (volume II of the Faral edition) is a frequently tedious but lucid account of the events that separate Baldwin's coronation from the death of Boniface de Montferrat (1204–1207): the conquest of Thrace; the dispute between Baldwin and Boniface over the possession of Thessalonica; Baldwin's death at the hands of Johanis of Bulgaria; the coronation of Henry of Flanders as second Latin emperor; Henry's war against Johanis; and the death of Boniface, killed by the Bulgars in September 1207.

Throughout his account, Villehardouin argues vigorously that the failure on the part of many crusading barons and their soldiers to assemble at Venice in 1202, as the treaty with the Venetians had stipulated a year earlier, set off an unavoidable chain of events that resulted in the change of course of the crusade from its original destination of Saracen Egypt to Constantinople. Impeded in their sincere attempt to honor their financial engagements with the Venetians because of the betrayal of "those who sailed from other ports," so the argument goes, the crusaders who sailed from Venice were compelled to help the Venetians in their conquest of Zara (a city on the Dalmatian coast long coveted by the doge) and to accept a plan submitted by the young refugee, prince Alexius Angelus, that would restore his imprisoned father, Isaac, to his rightful throne as emperor of Constantinople, provided Isaac were later to participate in the crusade.

More than a century ago Natalis de Wailly was the first to inquire whether Villehardouin was telling the story of the Fourth Crusade as he knew it, and much critical ink has flowed either to support or to challenge Villehardouin's sincerity.[2] Whether or not Villehardouin knew of a secret pact between the Venetians and the Sultan of Cairo; whether or not he knew, even before the Fourth Crusade was under way, that its real destination was Constantinople; whether or not he was aware of Dandolo's designs on the Byzantine city, no one has as yet been able to ascertain. The following pages will not resolve this problem, but they will attempt to detect concealed emotional charges, "blind spots," and unguarded revelations. In apologetic or confessional works of literature, verbal idiosyncracies and tones of voice can be as significant as the facts themselves—the most defensive part of the author's testimony.

No account of the Fourth Crusade can afford to overlook Robert de Clari (ca. 1170–after 1216), a footsoldier who accompanied Pierre d'Amiens and Hugues de Saint Pol on the Fourth Crusade. His brief account of the expedition, *Those Who Conquered Constantinople,* written from the fighting man's point of view, provides an important cross reference in order to verify or refute Villerhardouin's account.[3] It is significant, perhaps even symbolic, that Robert brought back from his trip to Constantinople a number of religious relics to the artistic value of which he was totally indifferent—significant in that he managed to reduce his moral conscience to silence and justify, at least to himself, one of the most curious chapters in the history of medieval plunder; symbolic in that, unlike Villehardouin and other leaders of the expedition, Robert does not seem to have realized the importance or to have foreseen the consequences of his actions. His brief chronicle is wrapped in a shroud of insuperable ignorance. He participated in none of the great decisions; he did not know that the plan to attack Constantinople had been hatched since or before the departure of the expedition from Venice; he knew nothing about the military strategy that had preceded the battles in which he fought, a lackluster and solipsistic figure; he knew nothing, finally, about the art works he plundered or the cities he helped devastate.

Villehardouin was intelligent enough to be a scoundrel. Robert could never have been more than an amiable Boeotian. Of doubts, hesitations, and moral misgivings he seems to have had few; but neither his moral conscience nor his sense of logic was sufficiently honed to permit him to arrive at any significant conclusions. He described the palaces, homes, churches, and abbeys of Constantinople with an engaging stupidity, and seemed unable to tell one proper noun from another. He was fascinated by certain Byzantine objects which he had never seen in France—the *buhotian,* for example, which the Byzantines used as an oxygen mask. His account of those who conquered Constantinople might easily have fallen into oblivion, an energetic but jumbled tale, but its worth lies in its momentary flashes of conscience that offer an embarrassing refutation to Villehardouin's glib and all too symmetrical apologetics.

Medieval scholars are usually either hostile or favorable to Villehardouin, and the author of *The Conquest of Constantinople* might, to a certain extent, be to blame for the controversy that surrounds his name. He is that sort of military chronicler who is forever dividing the world into two camps: the attacker without the walls and the defender within; those "who sail from Venice" and those "who sail from other ports"; those "who wish to disband the army" and those "who wish to keep it together"; those "whom God loves" and those "whom He ceases to love."[4] The Manichaean Villehardouin elicits Manichaean responses: perhaps that is why scholars feel compelled to take up the gauntlet of the debate that bears his name, either to defend his sincerity or to accuse him of concealing part of the truth about the altered destination of the Fourth Crusade from Egypt to Constantinople.

But perhaps that is not the only way to read *The Conquest of Constantinople.* If Villehardouin's chronicle were to be judged not as a historical document but as a literary creation dictated by a certain vision of reality, then the value of the work might depend entirely upon the artistic, intellectual, and moral qualities of the mind that produced it.[5] Villehardouin's chronicle tells the reader a good deal about the Fourth Crusade, but it incidentally tells him even more about the author's way of structuring his inner and outer vision. The problem of Villehardouin's sincerity has both a historical and a psychological sense; and, though it may perhaps never be possible to know whether Villehardouin was sincere in a factual sense, his language betrays a highly selective visual technique enabling the man quite literally to disregard whatever he consciously or unwittingly decides to exclude from his field of vision.

He seems to have been an eye witness to those moving sermons preached by the hermit Fulk of Neuilly, which open the chronicle. They were being attended by large audiences throughout the Ile de France and surrounding provinces—a convincing indication of the man's popular appeal. Success, whatever the enterprise, is an unmistakable sign of divine favor: "God worked many miracles," and Frenchmen throughout the Ile de France decide to enlist in the crusade preached by the hermit because of the generous terms of the indulgence promised by the papal legate to France: "Because this indulgence was so great, the hearts of the people were quite moved; and many enlisted because the indulgence was so great."[6]

In the spring of 1199, the barons assembled at Compiègne in order to decide when and from which port they would depart for *outremer*. In a familiar phrase, Villehardouin relates that "many points of view were put forward," but the essential outcome of the gathering was that he was one of six "best messengers" chosen to make final arrangements for the expedition, "with full power to settle what should be done, exactly as if they were their lords in person."[7]

At the age of fifty or so, Villehardouin was thus fulfilling what it is not presumptuous to call a lifelong ambition: to act and speak with the full power of a count. Villehardouin, the Marshal of Champagne, had the temporary privilege of acting and speaking like his master Thibaut de Champagne! One imagines him during that scenic if arduous trip on horseback from Compiègne to Venice wrapped entirely in thoughts of power and prestige. One must perforce imagine him thus, as he does not seem to have paused to record a single visual detail. A Froissart in the same circumstances would have riddled every Alpine innkeeper with questions, described every landscape, and collected every folktale along the way. Not so with Villehardouin. On such an important mission as this, he cannot afford to waste his time or disperse his attention: "The six messengers departed, . . . conferred among themselves, and decided that in Venice they were likely to find a greater number of ships than in any other port. And they journeyed on horseback in stages until they arrived at their destination the first week in Lent."[8]

Villehardouin's account of the treaty signed in 1201 with the Venetians is one of his finest pieces of factual reporting. When the aged doge, Enrico Dandolo, tells Villehardouin and his companions that they must wait four days before he can summon the members of his council and present the French requests, Villehardouin notes quite simply that "the envoys waited until the fourth day, as the doge had appointed and then returned to the palace, which was a most beautiful building and very richly furnished."[9] Like so much of Villehardouin's "bridge material," such an incidental remark might reveal more about the narrator's psychological and visual equipment than many of his more consciously florid passages. Had Villehardouin been endowed with great esthetic interest, would he not have paused at this point of his account, even a dozen years later, to describe his impressions of Venice during that four-day waiting period? But Villehardouin's is a practical, rather than a visual or speculative temper. To him, the act of seeing is a selective process and a preamble to action. Like a man of action, Villehardouin considers visual description a waste of time and energy. One is attentive to reality not in order to see it, but to act upon it. Inactive moments are spent not in dreams but in expectations: "They waited until the day he had fixed."[10]

Although shorn of visual interest, Villehardouin's account of the mission to Venice has an abstract geometric pattern. The doge's attempts to persuade the Venetian citizenry to grant the requests of the French envoys are drawn in concentric circles. First the doge is alone; four days later he presents the French proposals to his privy council, which approves them; three days later he summons his Grand Council, composed of forty of the wisest and most influential Venetian citizens; finally, "he brought them all to . . . approve and agree to accept the proposed covenant, . . . persuading first a few, then more, then still more, till at last all the members of his council expressed their approval and consent. After this he assembled a good ten thousand of the common people in the church of San Marco—the most beautiful church in the world—where he invited them to hear a Mass of the Holy Spirit, and pray to God for guidance concerning the request the envoys had made to them."[11]

Villehardouin sees reality more like an architect than a painter; like a strategist, he draws not with a brush but with a chalk and compass. Indeed, one is impressed in general by the poverty of Villehardouin's coloring, the one tint that seems worthy of his attention being vermilion.[12]

In a moving discourse at San Marco Villehardouin implores the people of Venice to take pity on Jerusalem and to join the French barons in the crusade. Then the six French envoys kneel at the feet of the crowd in tears. The doge and all the others cry out in a single voice, " 'We do agree! We do agree!' Then there was such a noise that it seemed as if the earth was falling. . . . When the great tumult had subsided, and this great show of pity, which surpassed anything that had ever been seen, the good duke of Venice, a very wise and courageous man, went up to the lectern and said to the people: 'My lords, see what an honor God has given us. . . .' I cannot recount all of the Duke's good and beautiful words."[13]

A memorable passage, but again how visually poor! How were the envoys dressed? Where were they kneeling? Where was the crowd standing? The reader must, like an imaginative archeologist, recreate the scene as if Villehardouin had provided a mere sketch or fragment. He must add epithets of color and sound to sentences that are almost entirely constructed with substantives and active verbs. Villehardouin's reluctance to recount "all of the duke's good words" reveals a distaste for digressive detail and an unquestionable talent for bringing out the inner meaning of an event, however biased the intepretation.

Villehardouin's habitual indifference to visual and intellectual nuance seems even more pronounced after the departure from Venice. The French barons have assembled at Venice in the spring of 1202, a year after the treaty with the Venetians. Of the eighty-five thousand marks requested by the Venetians for transporting the crusading army to Egypt, the barons have managed to a pay little better than fifty thousand, many of them having decided to sail from Flanders and Marseille. Perhaps Villehardouin is correct in arguing that it is the failure of all the barons to live up to the conditions of the treaty with Venice that compelled those who sailed from Venice to accept the altered course of the crusade.[14] His universe, in any case, is henceforth irrevocably divided between "those who sailed from Venice" and "those who sailed from other ports," and any action after the departure from Venice is motivated either by a treacherous desire to disband the army or by a patriotic attempt to keep it together. There can be no other way of seeing reality. Those who wish to disband the army are intended to resemble the fallen angels of a Manichaean heaven, even if their vision happens to have the greater number of adherents. Although the majority of the barons declare, at Venice, that they will shift for themselves and go some other way if the Venetians refuse to transport them to Egypt, Villehardouin suspects them of merely wishing to disband the army and return home. The enlightened, disinterested minority to which Villehardouin belongs is alone capable of acting nobly and in keeping with the divine mandates: "We'd much rather give all we have and go as poor men with the army than see it broken up and our enterprise a failure. For God will doubtless repay us in His own good time."[15]

As the chronicle progresses, Villehardouin's conscious selection of detail appears to grow more and more willfully systematic. One notices that he consistently views and represents reality in a contrast of light and shade which permits him to shape the contours of his narrative. His vision, in short, seems less a direct projection than a byproduct of contrasting light and shadow. With each advancing page, Villehardouin's "enlightened" viewpoint is forcefully, dogmatically projected against the foil of his adversaries' "dark" motives.

At Venice, in the summer of 1202, the leaders of the French army discover that, because many members of the crusading army have sailed from other ports, it will be impossible for them to pay the Venetians the full sum of money that was agreed upon at the treaty signed the year before. A few of the barons then propose that barons and foot-soldiers alike make up for the missing sum by contributing voluntarily of their money and goods. A majority of the crusaders argue against this proposal by stating that the sum they have already paid for their own passage is quite enough: "and if the Venetians are willing to take us, we're quite ready to go. If not we'll make shift for ourselves, and go some other way." Villehardouin cannot accept the good faith of such an argument and immediately accuses the majority of the crusaders of acting for some latent darker purpose: "They said this in actual fact, because they would have liked the army to be disbanded, and each man free to go home." Right after the meeting a few of the barons decide to set an example for the rest of the army by handing over all or most of their personal possessions to a common fund. Here Villehardouin describes the situation as a struggle between the niggling and destructive forces of darkness, who wish to disband the army, and the enlightened, disinterested few who share the narrator's opinion. And if it is the latter opinion that prevails, it is simply that God, "who gives hope to men in the depths of despair, was not willing" for the other side to have its way.[16]

Such a vision in black and white leads him to overdramatize the presence of the dark forces surrounding him and wishing him ill. Villehardouin is a master of the technique, well known to the professionally military, which consists of painting the darkest possible picture of what the enemy might do if he is not immediately wiped out. Hence the devastation and plunder of the Dalmatian city of Zara during the winter of 1203 is described as a "precaution" against the king of Hungary, to whom it belongs. Almost to reassure himself, Villehardouin adds dramatically "that the hearts of our people were not at peace, for one party was continually working to break up the army and the other to keep it together."[17] Surely such a "beautiful, prosperous and strongly defended" city as Zara could only be taken "with the help of God Himself!"[18]

Villehardouin's vision often loses all sense of perspective and proportion. Small objects are magnified and large ones made almost invisible. When Pope Innocent III excommunicates the barons for the crime of destroying the Christian city of Zara, his attitude is described merely as one of "displeasure."[19] The annihilation of the city by the Venetians, before the departure for Corfu, is described in a fleeting sentence: "The Venetians razed the city and its towers and walls."[20] Whereas the sight of a ravaged enemy city appears to be only a part of the logic of warfare, the defection from the army of several French barons is described much more strongly as "a great misfortune for the army, and a great disgrace to those who left it."[21] Villehardouin is adept at highlighting those events he wishes to dramatize. He is equally effective at blurring

or dimming the reader's vision of an event that might prove embarrassing, the assembly of the French barons at Zara, for example. The barons have just proposed to the army that if they help the young Alexius
Angelus reconquer the throne of Constantinople from his uncle, the
usurper Mourtzouphlos, he will bring the Byzantine empire back under
the religious jurisdiction of Rome, pay the French barons two hundred
thousand silver marks, and accompany the crusaders to Egypt with an
army of ten thousand men.[22] There follows "a great divergence of opinion in the assembly. The Cistercian abbot of Vaux had something to
say, in common with those who were eager to have the army disbanded.
They all declared they would never give their consent, since it would
mean marching against Christians. They had not left their home to do
any such thing, and for their part wished to go to Syria."[23] The abbot's
declaration makes one wonder why Villehardouin should then wish to
blur the clarity of the issues involved by adding that "there was discord
in the army. Nor can you wonder if the laymen were at loggerheads
when the Cistercians accompanying the forces were equally at variance
with each other."[24] The narrator thus subtly manages to blame the dis-
array of the army on the Cistercian abbots' confusion rather than on the
moral untenability of the barons' proposal. Rather than reproducing
reality, Villehardouin is creating an artificial windstorm of confusion,
presumably to make the reader infer either that the moral issues are
impossible to resolve or that the army is hopelessly divided.[25] The incidental minutiae will, Villehardouin seems to hope, blur the embarrassing conclusion that only twelve persons in all took the oaths on behalf
of the French; no more could be persuaded to come forward.[26]

The reader is left wondering by what juridical ploy a party of twelve
barons managed to decide the destiny of more than twenty thousand
crusaders. Rather than be forced to answer such a question, Villehardouin chooses immediately to distract the reader's attention to the great
number of desertions taking place: "During this time many men from
the lower ranks deserted and escaped in merchant ships. About five
hundred of them got away in one ship, but all of them lost their lives
by drowning. Another group escaped by land, thinking to travel safely
through Sclavonia; but the people of that country attacked them, killing
a great number, and those who were left came flying back to the army.
Thus our forces dwindled seriously from day to day."[27]

But the reader refuses to be distracted. How did the barons manage
to convince the army that the altered course to Constantinople was
morally acceptable? Strategists like Villehardouin know how useful tears
can be in reducing logical structures. Whether or not they are historically factual, tears serve to blur description and provide the chronicler

with an added excuse to heighten the dramatic nature of a critical moment: "The marquis [Boniface de Montferrat] and those with him fell at the feet of the other party, weeping bitterly, and said they would not get up again until these men had promised not to go away and leave them. . . . And when the others saw them they were filled with a great pity and wept sorely when they saw their lords, their relatives, and their friends fallen at their feet; and they said they would confer together and withdrew. Their decision was that they would remain with the army until Michaelmas, provided the leaders would solemnly swear on the gospels."[28]

Robert de Clari seems to have witnessed the same event with a drier eye:

> Then all the barons of the host were summoned by the Venetians. And when they were all assembled, the doge of Venice rose and spoke to them. "Lords," said the doge, "now we have a good excuse for going to Constantinople, if you approve of it, for we have the rightful heir." Now there were some who did not at all approve of going to Constantinople. Instead they said: "Bah! What shall we be doing in Constantinople? We have our pilgrimage to make, and also our plan of going to Babylon or Alexandria. Moreover, our navy is to follow us for only a year, and half of the year is already past." And the others said in answer: "What shall we do in Babylon or Alexandria when we have neither the provisions nor the money to enable us to go there? Better for us before we go there to secure provisions and money by some good excuse than to go there and die of hunger. . . ." And the marquis de Montferrat was at more pains to urge them to go to Constantinople than anyone else who was there, because he wanted to avenge himself for an injury for which the marquis hated the emperor of Constantinople. . . . Then the bishops answered that it would not be a sin but rather a righteous deed.[29]

The departure of the Franco-Venetian fleet from Corfu "on the eve of the Pentecost" (1203) is the most far-reaching and panoramic sight of Villehardouin's chronicle: "It seemed, indeed, that here was a fleet that might well conquer lands, for as far as the eye could reach there was nothing to be seen but sails outspread on all that vast array of ships, so that every man's heart was filled with joy at the sight."[30] Villehardouin, however, cannot help revealing himself even when enraptured. His visual attention is above all a process of exclusion ordained toward action; his joy at the sight of the fleet is neither an esthetic nor a moral response but an anticipation of action: "Here was a fleet that might well conquer lands." "There was nothing to be seen but sail outspread" is a curious admission that his visual field had excluded everything else. The common spectator like Robert de Clari knows that when a fleet like this lifts anchor, there is far more to be seen than sails outspread: "When the fleet left the port of Venice with its galleys, rich warships and so many other vessels, it was the most beautiful sight since the beginning of the world. For there were a hundred pairs of trumpets, made of silver as well as brass, sounding together at the weighing of the anchors, and so many bells and drums and other instruments that it was marvelous to behold. When the fleet was out to sea and had spread its sails and raised the banners and ensigns high on the masts, the whole sea seemed afire glittering with the ships upon it pouring out their joy."[31]

Villehardouin's exclusion of material unrelated to the action or purpose at hand applies to interior as well as exterior perceptions. At Cape Malia, in the southern Peloponnesus, the fleet happens to encounter two ships on their way back from Syria, "full of knights, sergeants, and pilgrims who were part of the company that had gone to that country by way of Marseille." Unwilling to trust the Venetians or to accept the mystifications of Boniface de Montferrat, these crusaders and the other barons had decided to sail directly for Syria. When they encountered the large fleet, a sergeant in one of the ships from Syria told his friends that he was going to join the expedition, "for it certainly seems to me they'll win some land for themselves."[32] Unable to resist the temptation to moralize, Villehardouin attributes the sergeant's gesture to a pious turn of heart: "And, after all, as people are wont to say, no matter how often a man can have gone astray, he can still come round to the right way in the end."[33] The comment does not seem to be made ironically, and it does not speak highly for Villehardouin's intuitions. It never seems to have occurred to the narrator that the sergeant's real motive might have been not to "come round to the right way" but to satisfy his appetite for gain. Such is one of the major paradoxes of Villehardouin's personality: his lucidity and intellectual rigor feed on truisms and reassuring platitudes. Even when he examines the human psyche he manages to exclude what he does not wish to see. Whether he is looking at the world or considering the arguments of those moral objectors "who wished to destroy the army," Villehardouin seems to see and hear only what his senses and his viewpoint care to admit.

When he first arrives within sight of Constantinople from the sea of Marmara, Villehardouin seems particularly impressed by such quantitative dimensions as the length, breadth, and height of the city: "I can assure you that all those who had never seen Constantinople before gazed very intently at the city, having never imagined there could be so fine a place in all the world. They noted the high walls and lofty towers encircling it, and its rich palaces and tall churches, of which there were so many that no one could have believed it to be true if he had not seen it with his own eyes, and viewed the length and breadth of that city which reigns supreme over all the others. There was indeed no man so brave and daring that his flesh did not shudder at the sight."[34]

Throughout his account of the siege and conquest of the city, Constantinople remains an object of eventual possession rather than of visual perception. One gathers the impression that the city is an abstract, two-dimensional configuration of lines being examined in headquarters, on a military map. Neither ships nor scaling ladders nor land nor sea nor horses are given any concrete dimensions; nor is the city viewed from a recognizable geographical perspective: "The Venetians were strongly of the opinion that the scaling ladders should be set up on the ships and the whole assault be made from the sea. The French, for their part, protested that they could not give such a good account of themselves on sea as the Venetians; but once on land, with their horses and their proper equipment, they could do much better service. So in the end it was decided that the Venetians would launch their attack from the sea while the barons and their army would tackle the enemy by land."[35]

Yet some of the scenes are recorded "live." The first of three great fires within the city's walls is observed from the shore opposite the port, near the tower of Galata, whence Villehardouin commands a broad and relatively close view of the city's walls: "The fire was so great and horrible that no one was able to extinguish or control it. When the barons in the camp on the other side of the port saw it, they were sorely afflicted, seeing the high churches and rich palaces crumble and collapse, and the great commercial quarters burn. . . . The fire spread beyond the port toward the most densely populated part of the city, until it reached the sea on one side near the church of Saint Sophia. . . . As it burned, the fire extended easily over a mile and a half of land."[36]

Villehardouin seems to be standing on the very same spot several months later as he watches the Venetians foil the Greeks' attempt to burn the crusading fleet:

> One night, at midnight, they set fire to their ships, hoisted the sails, and let the ships flame, so that it seemed as if the shore was on fire. The Greek ships floated toward the crusaders' fleet. The alarm went off in the camp. All ran to take up their arms. The Venetians and all those who owned ships scrambled to their ships and set about protecting them as best they could. And Geoffroy de Villehardouin, the Marshal of Champagne, who has composed this work, can testify that never did a seafaring people better manage than the Venetians. They

leaped into the galleys and rowboats of their ships, grappled the Greek ships with hooks, and pulled them with all their strength (while their enemies looked on) into the current of the sea of Marmara, and let them sail in flames down toward the sea. There were so many Greeks on the far shore that it was impossible to count them; and the din was so great that it seemed as if the earth and the sky were falling.[37]

When Constantinople is sacked by the army in April 1204, however, the chronicler's eye is distracted by the various foci of action and dispersed ubiquitously throughout the city:

The Marquis de Montferrat rode straight along the shore to the palace of Bucoleon. As soon as he arrived there the place was surrendered to him. . . . In the same way that the palace of Bucoleon was surrendered to the Marquis de Montferrat, so the palace of Blachernae was yielded to the Comte de Flandre's brother Henri, and on the same conditions. . . . There too was found a great store of treasure, not less than there had been in the palace of Bucoleon. . . . The rest of the army, scattered throughout the city, also gained much booty; so much, indeed, that no one could estimate its amount or its value. It included gold and silver, table-services and precious stones, satin and silk, mantles of squirrel fur, ermine and miniver, and every choicest thing to be found on this earth. Geoffroy de Villehardouin here declares that, to his knowledge, so much booty had never been gained in any city since the creation of the world. . . . So the troops of the crusaders and the Venetians . . . all rejoiced and gave thanks to our Lord for the honour and the victory he had granted them . . . so that those who had been poor now lived in wealth and luxury.[38]

But even this, one of the most large-scale of Villehardouin's pictures, excludes all embarrassing detail. Without going so far as to recall Delacroix's flamboyant recreation of the sack of the city, one has only to read the contemporary Byzantine chronicler Nicetas Choniates in order to realize that Villehardouin's picture is a whitened one indeed:

The lust of the army spared neither maiden nor the virgin dedicated to God. Violence and debauchery were everywhere present; cries and lamentations and the groans of the pilgrims were heard throughout the city; for everywhere pillage was unrestrained and lust unbridled. The city was in wild confusion. Nobles, old men, women, and children ran to and fro trying to save their wealth, their honor, and their lives. Knights, foot-soldiers, and Venetian sailors jostled each other in a mad scramble for plunder. Threats of ill treatment, promises of safety if wealth were disgorged, mingled with the cries of many sufferers. These pious brigands . . . acted as if they had received a licence to commit every crime.[39]

So complex, so morally embarrassing is the event that Villehardouin must fall back upon his habitual defenses of selection and distraction to describe it. Selection of visual detail is a rather easy process: one simply excludes what one does not wish to see. But how does the writer distract the reader's attention when describing the climactic event of a chronicle? By overdramatizing the dangers of the situation and creating a "new enemy." To the ranks of those iniquitous sons of darkness who had "sailed from other ports," of those enemies "who wished to disband the army," of those Byzantine Greeks who did the French army so much harm by attempting to defend their own city, Villehardouin adds a fourth group of enemies, the soldiers within the crusading army who refused to surrender their plunder to the barons: "Some performed this duty conscientiously; others, prompted by covetousness, that never-failing source of all evil, proved less honest."[40]

His Manichaean world is henceforth divided between the "righteous" sackers of cities, who dutifully surrender their spoils, and the "unrighteous," who try to keep theirs: "From the very first, those who were prone to this vice began to keep some things back and became, in consequence, less pleasing to our Lord. Ah! God, how loyally they had behaved up to now! And up to now, in all their undertakings, our Lord had shown his gracious care for them and had exalted them above all people. But those who do right often have to suffer for the misdeeds of the unrighteous."[41]

The second half of Villehardouin's chronicle is a tedious recitation of the battles fought between those who do right and those who do wrong, of new enemies either defeated or victorious. "Such an arduous task it was to found the Latin empire in Greece," he might have concluded with a Vergilian turn of phrase, "when so many enemies were opposed to the designs of providence: Greeks, Wallachians, Bulgars, not to mention the dissident factions within the conquering army!" The chronicler's account of the events that occur between the election of Baldwin of Flanders as emperor of Constantinople (May 1204) and the death of Boniface de Montferrat (September 1207) is a dry enumeration of sieges, battles, and conquests in Thrace, on the Greek Mainland, in the Peloponnesus, and in Asia Minor. It is almost as if Villehardouin himself found the events that followed the sack of the city to be anticlimactic and hardly worth the reader's interest.

After the conquest Villehardouin never so much as alludes to the possibility of a departure for *outremer*. So much has happened since Venice that the reader will (one hopes) have forgotten that the expedition originally began as a crusade against the Infidel. The account of the events of 1204–1207 is but a prolonged distraction intended to discourage the reader from inquiring why, after conquering the city and liquidating their debt with the Venetians, the French barons thought it necessary to conquer the entire Greek empire rather than get down to the business of continuing the crusade.

Selection, discoloration, exclusion, dramatization, obfuscation of issues, distraction—such are a few of the major components of Villehardouin's narrative technique. Though it would be presumptuous to argue that a study of this technique allows one to bring a definitive answer to the "Villehardouin debate," it does seem to permit an evaluation of it. Historians will perhaps never know whether Villehardouin willfully concealed some facts as to the origins of the Fourth Crusade; but his visual and psychic makeup were such that, had he known these facts, he would probably have selected them carefully and rigorously. Can one conclude otherwise when one sees him so selective in depicting even harmless and unembarrassing events?

Approaching the problem of Villehardouin's sincerity by way of narrative technique serves the further purpose of providing a different opinion of the author's character. One fails to see that "mixture of simplicity and nobility that are characteristically his."[42] One finds it hard to respond to those "energetic, adventurous, rough and loyal spirits of the conquerors of Constantinople," or those "tears of pity" that Sainte-Beuve praises in a highly rhetorical passage.[43] One finds it impossible, finally, to agree with Edmond Faral's all too flattering picture of Villehardouin the loyal and courageous soldier.[44]

Such glorified images of Villehardouin are perhaps better discarded. Of his love of courage it can surely be said that he admired it selectively, in those who happened to share his views; and it might be argued that his "rough and loyal" character is largely the product of his selective perceptions. Villehardouin strikes some readers as a man of immoderate ambition whose talent for discourse and political compromise was largely self-serving. His fascination for wealth, plunder, and reputation impoverished his better impulses; despite his wealth of experience, his visual memory remains poor, rough, and discolored; the result is a sketchy, unshaded, and curiously defensive picture of the most important event of his age.

3 JOINVILLE: HISTORY AS CHIVALRIC CODE

VILLEHARDOUIN's chronicle was composed a short time after the events narrated in order to justify a series of decisions the morality or the opportunity of which had been brought into question by some of his contemporaries. The circumstances surrounding the composition of Joinville's biography of Saint Louis are quite different. While Villehardouin was writing in a spirit of self-righteousness on a debatable subject, Joinville wrote in a spirit of reminiscence about a king whom the Roman Catholic Church, less than thirty years after his death, was in the process of canonizing.

Born in early 1225, Joinville was ten years younger than Saint Louis.[1] After the premature death of his oldest brother and of his father, Joinville inherited his ancestral home, which had belonged to his family since the eleventh century. When King Louis took the cross in 1244, after a prolonged illness, Joinville immediately and enthusiastically followed suit. He sailed with the crusading fleet from the port of Hyères in southern France, followed the king to Cyprus, and took part in the landing at Damietta and in the battle of Mansourah in July 1248. Like King Louis, he was captured soon after this battle by the Bedouins and spent several months in a prison at Mansourah. Only by dint of a large ransom paid by the king did he and Louis avoid being decapitated.

After their release from prison, Joinville settled with the king on the Syrian coast. At Acre, in 1250, he argued vehemently against those barons in the king's council who favored an immediate return to France. For four years, from 1250 until 1254, he lived close to Louis at Acre, Caesarea, and Jaffa, served him as counselor and steward, and sailed

41

with him back to France in July 1254. Back at his ancestral home, Joinville led a quiet, sedentary life until his death in 1317.

The Seventh Crusade had marked him for the rest of his life. His decision, in 1267, not to accompany Louis IX to Tunis for what was destined to be the king's final crusade was taken firmly and irrevocably. Religious though he was, Joinville found that the crusade of 1248 had been enough for his tastes. So alive were his memories of those cruel years that shortly after 1272 he began writing a personal account of the events of 1248–54. No doubt he did not realize at the time that he was in fact writing the body of what was later to become the *History of Saint Louis*. When, around 1298, Jeanne de Navarre, the young wife of King Philippe le Bel, begged Joinville to compose "a book containing the holy words and good deeds of Saint Louis," Joinville completed his manuscript, binding it at both ends with introductory and concluding chapters in praise of Saint Louis's Christian virtues, particularly his sense of charity and justice.

Joinville's vision of events has been described as laudatory, nostalgic, natural, sincere. Some of his critics have praised his extraordinary visual memory, while others say it already showed traces of senility. Rarely, perhaps, has a classic been so widely praised and so loosely analyzed. No one has ever paid attention to the negative side of Joinville's vision: the overt or implicit criticisms of Louis IX, the things left unsaid. Joinville's rhetorically modest claim in the opening passage to be writing merely in response to a pious queen's wish to revive the memory of her husband's grandfather has all too often been accepted at face value. The fact that he finished his book several years after the death of the queen whose request had set the work in motion should itself be an indication that Joinville's purpose transcended the vain wish to add yet another title to the list of the tediously flattering lives of Saint Louis that were published during the generation following the king's death.[2]

Readers of Joinville's *History of Saint Louis* like to recall the incidents in Chapter 4 as they do a familiar child's tale. Like a children's story, the scene might easily be represented with a series of Epinal pictures—those polychrome, heavily stylized images which for generations have provided French schoolchildren with an introduction to sweetened versions of their past. Chapter 4 of Joinville's chronicle seems to contain, as in a capsule, characteristic medieval attitudes toward social relationships, toward problems of dogmatic and moral theology, and toward the relative value of the present life in its relationship with the hereafter.

The actors perform with a curious mixture of flowing grace and puppetlike awkwardness; the liquidity of their gestures and words is sometimes broken up by gauche hesitations and trite pronouncements; like the smiling angel of the cathedral of Rheims, they strike a rigid pose, yet at the same time they give off flickers of warmth and sparks of humor. Louis IX has summoned his seneschal for a discussion of one of the most central of theological issues. He is aware of Joinville's dialectical subtlety ("I hesitate to speake to you of what touches God, for I know the subtlety of your mind"), and not entirely sure of his own capacities for argument and refutation; he has therefore chosen to protect himself by inviting a pair of friars to sustain him should he suffer a theological lapse in Joinville's presence. Louis's first question concerns the quiddity of God: "Tell me, Seneschal, what sort of a thing is God?" Joinville's reply amounts to a layman's version of Saint Anselm's ontological proof: "God is something so good that there cannot be any better." For his "excellent" answer, Joinville is rewarded with the king's unqualified approval, "for the very words in which you answered are written in this book I hold in my hand."[3]

Wishing to test Joinville further, Louis asks him two other questions, realizing perhaps that Joinville, with his distaste for every form of excess, will have trouble in providing a "correct" answer: whether Joinville would prefer to be a leper or to have committed a mortal sin; whether he washes the feet of the poor on Maundy Thursday. To the former question, Joinville retorts that he would rather commit thirty mortal sins than become a leper, and to the latter he answers simply: "God forbid!" The king dismisses the second answer as "wild and foolish" and the third as "poor."

For centuries readers have smiled or chortled over this confrontation and have assumed that Joinville is consciously playing the King's fool. One assumes that Joinville, as the king's seneschal, wants to act as a foil to what he considers the king's excessive seriousness. Upon closer examination, however, one sees Joinville and Louis IX differently. It is not at all certain that the seneschal wishes to play the fool. There are several scenes in the *History of Louis IX* when it is Joinville who has the last word, the punch line, the courageous piece of advice, or the word of reproval, where it is the king who ends up looking foolish. Any careful reader will notice that Joinville is as serious as is Louis himself about such matters as war, death, Christian piety, and salvation. Even in the scene just referred to, Joinville nowhere indicates that the king is right; nowhere does he say that Louis's answer is irrefutable or that he finds it convincing. Quite diplomatically, he chooses to drop the matter and say nothing further. (Nevertheless one may imagine Joinville after the scene, feeling somewhat amused but undaunted.)

This scene is less comic, far more dramatic than French schoolmasters have traditionally presented it to their students over the centuries. The décor has all the plainness of a school or courtroom braced for theological or juridical debate. The characters belong to the only two social classes that might be expected to have a smattering of high culture: the nobility and the clergy. Each of the members present is aware of his social rank. Each knows that, no matter what the outcome of the debate, social stratification will under no circumstances be altered. The king, it will be noticed, has asserted his authority by calling the debate and even setting the rules by which the game will be played. The seneschal, a king's steward, has no other choice but to accept or reject the game. The friars, like the book on the king's knees, are symbolic of intellectual and spiritual authority. But how unobtrusive they are! They are dismissed as quickly as they had been summoned, without adding a word to the conversation, as if Louis IX simply wants to provide them (and perhaps his seneschal) with a physical reminder of their allegiance to him in social and temporal matters.

Suddenly, almost without warning, the scene becomes what Louis had from the start expected it to be: a personal confrontation, a testing of will rather than intellect, between himself and a subordinate, between a king and a member of the feudal nobility. Louis IX seems, in fact, to be consciously raising an issue that has obsessed all his Capetian forebears since Philip I: that in any confrontation between king and feudal nobility it is the principle of hereditary monarchy that must win.

Joinville has passed the test of intellect with an excellent answer. He is clearly intended to lose the test of will. Questions two and three cannot, in point of fact, be answered with a right or wrong answer. If he is to be sincere Joinville can only reply to both of these conundrums with a statement of personal preference or taste. Yet Louis IX reprimands him as if in both cases he has given a wrong answer. He mildly humiliates his seneschal by making him sit at his feet as he plays the role of severe master chastising a bad pupil. But Joinville is in no mood to be chastised. Sitting at the king's feet, after the dismissal of the friars, he tells Louis that he is "still of the same mind." When Louis insists that his is a "wild and roguish way of speaking" and lapses into a bland monologue about the relative merits of leprosy and mortal sin, Joinville does the only thing a civilized feudal lord can do when he is reduced to silence by the first noble in the kingdom: he speaks no further. But nowhere does Joinville concede that the king's answer is right.

The text of Chapter 4 first appears to the reader as just another illustration of the high sanctity of a man to whom Joinville's earthy humanity is supposed to act as foil. In fact it is a rapid encounter of clashing opinions, quickly followed by a troubled silence. Set up by Louis IX as a theological game in the presence of the clergy, the confrontation is quickly transformed into a symbolic test of will between a king and his seneschal in the solitude of the king's closet. After the seneschal has twice asserted an opinion that is diametrically opposed to the king's, he listens passively but refuses to capitulate as the king symbolically reminds him of his social inferiority and sternly reaffirms his moral authority.

Close inspection reveals the entire *History of Saint Louis* to be filled with ambiguities like these. The author's performance belies his stated intentions, and the hagiographical halo that has been placed above the book for centuries simply refuses to glow. For example, in the opening paragraphs Joinville claims that he has divided his book into two parts: "The first part tells how he ordered himself at all times by the will of God and of the Church, and for the well-being of his Kingdom; the second part of the book treats of the great things he did as a knight and a soldier" (1, 2). But the book is clearly divided into three sections: a first (chapters 1–24) highlighting some of the privileged moments of the king's life; a mammoth middle section (chapters 25–134), the main subject of which is Joinville's eyewitness account of the Seventh Crusade of 1248–54 and of his participation in that crusade alongside the king; and a final section (chapters 135–49), again dedicated to the highlights of Louis's life (especially after the Seventh Crusade), with much of the material being borrowed from contemporary biographies or chronicles.[4]

Structural analysis of the text has, to a certain extent, provided a satisfactory reason for Joinville's failure to live up to his intention of writing an edifying two-part biography of King Louis. Scholars now agree that Joinville stated his intentions long after most of the book had been written, as the body of the book was intended to be not so much hagiographical as autobiographical. Around 1272, perhaps on the occasion of the marriage of his eldest son to Mabile de Villehardouin, Joinville began to compose his personal reminiscences of the crusade of 1248–54, his model for which was the chronicle written by the scion of the illustrious family into which his son was marrying. No one knows what became of that early biography of Joinville, nor whether it was ever circulated. Several years later Queen Jeanne of Navarre begged Joinville to write a book on "the holy words and good deeds of our king Saint Louis." "It would seem likely," writes Joan Evans, "that she made this request at some time before 1297, when the King was canonized, from the desire to have all the possible evidence in favour of canonization that was to bring peculiar honour to the Royal House."[5] René Hague has argued that the autobiographical part of Joinville's history was written around or before 1272, and that the hagiographical part was written sometime between 1272 and 1309.[6]

Perhaps no one will ever know for sure what the original version of Joinville's autobiography looked like. The author is plainly the central character of the final version, with Louis IX playing an essential but ancillary role. Yet Joinville's book has always been considered above all a book on the sanctity of King Louis. Why does this cleavage exist between what Joinville plainly says and what generations have always thought him to mean?

One might dismiss this as a pseudoproblem; or reply that, though Joinville allows himself more space, Louis IX remains the central figure; or assume that the discrepancy between intention and execution is largely a technical matter due to the fact that the author, not a professionally trained writer, completed his book without realizing that the bulk of its autobiographical materials all but succeeded in crowding the hagiographical materials out of the picture. Whether the asymmetry of the book and its failure to live up to the claims set forth in the preface can be ascribed to oversight, to old age, or to haste in completing the final product, one fact stands out: it is impossible to maintain that the book is what it purports to be, a book about the sanctity of Louis IX.

One thus remains inclined to assert that this is not a pseudoproblem and that the explanation does not reside in incompetence or old age or a hasty compilation of materials written several decades apart. If Joinville's book, as published, turns out to be anything but what the title and the prologue proclaim it to be, may it not be that Joinville's oversights, like his preteritions, are intended to be meaningful? May it not be that Joinville knew what he was about and that beneath the avowed purposes of the book he is in fact pointing obliquely toward an implicit conclusion?

The *History of Saint Louis* is a highly class-conscious book, none of the protagonists being more class-conscious than the author himself. Several anecdotes in the story illustrate to what extent Joinville was imbued with all the prejudices of his class, perhaps none more illuminating than Joinville's brief conversation with Robert de Sorbon, a member of the lower class who had managed to win his way into the king's entourage. To "Master Robert," who has just suggested to him that wearing finer clothes than the king is equivalent to "sitting above him on the bench," Joinville drily replies: "saving your grace, Master Robert, I am in no way to be blamed for wearing green and ermine. It was my father and mother who left me this gown. It is you who are in the wrong; you are the son of working folk [*vilains*] and you have given up the clothes your father and mother wore and are dressed in finer woolen cloth than the King." Louis IX, incidentally, is called to witness this dialogue, and his presence, characteristically, transforms it into a test of strength between the two nobles, "the King arguing in Robert's defence with the greatest vigour" (6, 36).

Joinville recalls admiringly how Count Henry the Generous of Champagne, having encountered a knight begging on the steps of Saint Stephen's Church at Troyes and not being able to express his fabled generosity in specie, did so in kind by giving away his companion, the burgher Artaud of Nogent. He did so, however, not without reminding the burgher of his inferior status: "Sir Villain," said the count, turning to Artaud, "you are wrong in saying that I have nothing more to give; I have you." Joinville adds, quite casually, that the knight took Artaud by the cloak and told him that he would not release him until the burgher had paid a ransom; "and before he was freed Artaud paid up to the tune of five hundred pounds" (20, 90–92).

In Egypt, and again in Caesarea, during the crusade of 1248–54, Joinville thought it natural that the common folk of the French army should set up a brothel at a stone's throw from the king's tent, and he expresses some measure of surprise that the king should dismiss them for having indulged in such sport. What, after all, are common yokels expected to do during their idle hours?[7] On the other hand, Joinville deems it "disgraceful" for a knight to talk and laugh while mass is being sung for the repose of the soul of a fellow knight (69, 297–98). He refuses adamantly and angrily to overlook the fact that one of his knights has been bullied by one of the king's men-at-arms and threatens to leave the king's service if he does not receive satisfaction, "seeing that . . . men-at-arms could push knights about" (99, 509). And Joinville's way of dispensing and rationing wine to his inferiors in Caesarea was directly related to their position on the social scale: "I bought a hundred barrels of wine, of which I always had the best drunk first. The servants' wine I had mixed with water, the squires' with less water. At my own table the knights were served with a large flask of wine and another of water, so that they could mix it to their taste" (98, 503–504).

Louis IX himself displays much the same caste prejudice as his seneschal. Though it may seem contentious to say so, the king's way of waiting upon "his poor" at table, giving them money before sending them on their way, and washing their feet on Maundy Thursday has a paternalistic and cloying odor about it. Other incidents in the narrative illustrate Louis's sense of social decorum and his belief in the unalterability of the orders of society. To the count of Montfort, who has been solidly outclassed in theological debate with a Jew, Louis suggests that lay noblemen should leave theological debates to the "learned clerks," the nobleman's business being, "as soon as he hears the Christian faith maligned, [to] defend it only by the sword, with a good thrust in the belly, as far as the sword will go" (10, 50–53). The king is refreshingly merciless when he is quibbling with the clergy or the hierarchy over social or political matters and uses the strongest language to remind them of their social rank.[8] Unfortunately, however, his strongest verbal lashings, his cruelest punishments, seem to be reserved for burghers or *vilains*. A knight caught in a brothel in Caesarea is allowed to choose either to forfeit his horse or to be led through the camp by his whore with a cord tied round his genitalia, but a goldsmith caught "uttering a filthy oath" is "put in the pillory, in his shirt and drawers, with the guts and lights of a pig round his neck, such a heap of them that came right up to his nose" (138, 685).[9] And it was a Parisian burgher whose nose and lips the king allegedly branded because he too had uttered a filthy oath.[10] Did Louis consider prostitution such a lesser sin than cursing that he should punish it so lightly, almost humorously? Or is the sin different according to whether the sinner is a noble, a knight, a burgher, a tradesman? And what is the reader to think of the king's harsh reply to Joinville's demand for indulgence toward Ponce, the old squire, who has served three generations of kings: "Seneschal . . . he has not served us. It is we that have served him, by allowing him to stay with us in spite of his bad habits" (133, 662)? The remainder of the king's reply sounds far less characteristic of a saint than of an advocate of free enterprise telling his son the secret of his family's success in business: "My grandfather King Philip told me that in rewarding your servants you should give one more and one less, according to their service. And he used to say also that no man could govern a country well if he could not refuse as boldly and bluntly as he could give. I tell you this . . . because people are now so greedy in their demands that there are few who look to the salvation of their souls and the honour of their persons, so long as they can by right or wrong lay their hands on other people's property."

For both Joinville and Saint Louis, in short, society was still pretty much composed of three basic orders: nobility, clergy, and peasant or burgher (*preudomes, clercs, vilains*). Ever since the time of Augustine, social orders had been described, and social duties apportioned, in such threefold terms. There are those who uphold the faith with the sword, the *defensores;* those who uphold it with discourses and prayer, the *clerici* or *oratores;* and those whose business is to work, both for self-preservation and for the perpetuation of the classes above them, the *laboratores.*[11] The vision of the social order held by Joinville and the king could have been held by any citizen of the later empire or of the feudal age: Augustine, Cassiodorus, Boethius, Charlemagne, Hugues Capet, Philip I, or Louis VII. The essential thing for a Christian, as Saint Paul had so clearly said, was to know his social *ordo* and stick to it: "in the state in which he was called" (*I Cor.* VII:20). For Joinville and Louis IX, class consciousness meant the art of holding one's rank as best one could; and living up to the highest ideal of that rank meant being a *preudome.*

What does it mean to be *preudome?*[12] The question is twice raised in Joinville's chronicle. On the first occasion (5, 32), the concept of *preudomie* is set apart from that of *beguinage,* the life of the devout layman living a religious life in community. For Louis, a *preudome* is "better than a beguin." That is to say, a lay Christian devoting himself heart and soul to the "defense and illustration" of the Christian religion in the world is better than a lay Christian who devotes himself to a life of surrogate monasticism: "When we had been disputing for a long time, the king gave his finding. . . . 'I would dearly love to have the name of being a *preudome* so long as I deserved it, and you would be welcome to the rest. For a *preudome* is so grand and good a thing that even to pronounce the word fills the mouth pleasantly' " (5, 32).

Later, in a digressive historical flashback, Joinville recalls a distinction once made, during the Third Crusade, by the "great King Philip" (Philip Augustus) about one of his men whom he considered physically brave but unworthy of the title of *preudome:*

> There is a world of difference [said King Philip] between a brave man [*preu home*] and a brave and good man [*preudome*]. There are, in Christians and Saracen lands, many brave knights, who have never believed in God and His Mother. And that is why I say that God gives a great gift and a great grace to the Christian knight whom he permits both to be bodily brave and to be His servant, preserving him from mortal sin; and it is the man who so orders himself that one should call *preudome,* since his prowess is a gift from God. But those of whom I spoke before, one should call *preuz homes,* since they are physically brave, but take no heed either of God or of sin. (109, 559–60)

Preudomie, therefore, appears to be a mean of excellence situated somewhere between an escapist piety and an impious audacity. The *preudome,* of necessity, is a layman, a Christian, an active and courageous participant in the affairs of the world, if need be a warrior and "defensor fidei"; he is not a *beguin* in that he eschews neither fine clothes nor gaiety nor the affairs of court nor worldly honor nor even the throne of his kingdom; but though he is physically brave, he "believes in God and His Mother" and is chary of committing mortal sins. He is "both bodily brave and a servant of God." One might say of him what Aristotle said of his proud men: "it is honour that they chiefly claim, but in accordance with their deserts," provided one adds that "he acknowledges God as the source of all honor and the end of all his service."[13]

Preudomie, it should be stressed, was a layman's ideal. Joinville realized that it was an ideal open to the Christian by the mere fact that he had not chosen the life of the cloister; and he certainly found it difficult (as Joan Evans suggests) "to accept the truth that the *prud'homme* was noble by character but not necessarily by birth."[14] I would go yet further and suggest that, so far as Joinville is concerned, the implicit conclusion to be drawn from his memoirs is that *preudomie* is an ideal open to the nobility alone. The *preudome* is a noble who has reached his peak of excellence. To Robert de Sorbon, the "son of working folk," Joinville concedes no more than "the great reputation he had for being a *preudome*" ("la grant renommée qu'il avoit d'estre preudome"), and for this the king allowed him to eat at his table (5, 37).[15] But it was only a matter of reputation, and Joinville was the first to remind Master Robert of his humble origins whenever the latter forgot the fact that at the king's board he was simply a *déclassé.* Never does Joinville ascribe the title of *preudome* to a clerk or a *vilain* (Master Robert being one only by adoption); but the king's eight counselors, as well as the lords who accompanied Louis and Joinville on the crusade are referred to as *preudomes* without qualification.[16]

A *preudome* simply because he belonged to the one class for which this ideal was conceivable, Joinville considered himself a social equal of Louis IX. *"Singulariter,"* he might have said, in scholastic discourse, "I am the king's seneschal; but *specialiter,* I am his social peer." As an individual, Joinville was the king's inferior; as a member of the nobility he was the king's class peer. Many times in his account the sentiment— one is almost tempted to say the resentment—of equality (a feudal resentment somewhat diluted by the middle of the thirteenth century, but never entirely repressed) is clearly implied.

Joinville's qualifications for the ideal of *preudomie* had a firm genealogical base. His first and last preoccupation before leaving for the crusade of 1248 is to spend a week with his family, "putting things right," as he describes it, and settling all matters of his estate (25, 111). For a full week before his departure, he plays the role of *paterfamilias,* feasting and dancing with his family, his brother the lord of Vaucouleurs, "and other great men." During that week, his first wife, the sister of the count of Grandpré, gives birth to Joinville's son John, lord of Ancerville, and Joinville is reassured by the thought that a male descendant will perpetuate the family name while he is abroad on his long and dangerous mission (25, 110). When he takes leave of his estate, having bequeathed most of his worldly possessions to his heirs, he does not dare look back, "lest my heart should weaken at the thought of the lovely castle I was leaving and of my two children" (28, 122).

The disasters and humiliations of the Egyptian campaign make Joinville no less conscious of his superior origin than before. In the full swing of his first landing on the shores of Damietta, in Egypt, he notes that the count of Jaffa "of the house of Joinville . . . made the finest landing of all" (34, 158). At Mansourah, where he is made captive, he is nearly assassinated by a Saracen who takes him for the king's cousin. When he succeeds in proving that he is related through his mother to Emperor Frederick of Germany, his life is spared. The Saracens are visibly impressed to hear that Joinville is a grandnephew of Frederick Barbarossa. "Otherwise," he comments with laconic grace, "we should all have been killed" (65, 326).

Joinville had every right to consider himself as the equal, in social class, of King Louis. He seems to have exercised that right unstintingly, as is obvious from his account of the occasions when he did not hesitate to speak up to his master; and when Saint Louis seems to have the last word, never will the reader find Joinville explicitly admitting defeat. Many are the occasions, on the other hand, when Joinville might have claimed to score a point, had his game of one-upmanship with Louis IX been explicitly declared. Why is he so emphatic in saying that, though he was severely outnumbered, it was he who prevailed upon Louis IX to remain in Caesarea rather than return prematurely to France (84–85)? Why the demeaning details about the king's dysentery at Mansourah ("so bad that it was necessary, so often was he obliged to go to the latrine, to cut away the lower part of his drawers"), while Joinville's illness from a throat tumor is described in dignified if melodramatic detail?[17] Why, within earshot of the king, does Joinville speak so compassionately with the renegade Christian who has converted to Islam, whom the king has just contemptuously told to be on his way (71, 418)? Why is Joinville so deliberately sanguine in telling of the gambling habits of the king's brothers at Acre (71, 418) while he stresses the king's intolerance and fury at the sight of their dicing (79, 405)? Why does Joinville address himself with such mock deference to the king when the pilgrims from Greater Armenia ask the seneschal to allow them into the king's tent, that they might see the "holy King":

"I do not want to kiss your bones just yet" (110, 566)? Why does Joinville dwell on details such as the king's "estrangement" from his hapless wife Marguerite, his excessive and "senseless" grief after the death
of his mother, his abnormal oedipal tendencies, his morbid and mother-
inherited fear of sin (116, 594; 119, 604–608)?

Why? Because Louis IX answered only imperfectly to Joinville's mature and quite personal idea of Christian *preudomie*. One doubts whether
such an intelligent writer as the old seneschal, whose experience of life
was certainly as extensive as the king's, could fully admire the much-
vaunted "sanctity" of a man for whom committing a mortal sin seems
one and the same thing as desecrating his own mother. One doubts, too,
whether Joinville truly admired the king's jejune way of presenting matters of faith in terms of conundrums and catechismal games ("Now, dear
man, which would you prefer, leprosy or mortal sin?"). Such suspicions
and doubts are perhaps not fully subject to proof. One cannot demon-
strate what Joinville really thought about matters toward which he had
to keep a diplomatic silence, even years after the king's canonization:
or better, especially after the king's canonization, when the legend of
the king's sanctity was rampant throughout the kingdom. One can only
infer some of Joinville's authentic feeling toward Louis IX from his
innuendos, his sallies of humor, and his silences. To pretend that Joinville's overt admiration for Louis IX was merely a cover for hostility
would, of course, be overstating the case. It seems likely, however, that
the seneschal considered his king as, at best, a *primus inter pares,* perhaps a "sanctus inter pares," but no more; and there are moments when
he unquestionably considered himself more faithful to the canons of
preudomie than the king himself.

This is not to say that Joinville ever thought of himself as a superior
preudome, but simply that, to his mind, Louis occasionally betrayed
that ideal either by excess or by default. Joinville's conception of *preudomie* is a balanced ideal, a mean of excellence, a state of moral equilibrium which, paradoxically, demands the fullest of the Christian lord's
powers. Any excess in the striving for *preudomie* yields a lesser, not a
greater sum of virtue. Any excess, even in the defense of the faith, yields
less *preudomie,* therefore less sanctity. For *preudomie* is neither more
nor less, in Joinville's mind, than lay Christian sanctity. Little wonder,
then, that King Louis himself considered it far preferable to be a *preudome* than a *beguin: preudomie* simply corresponded better to the ideal
of sanctity that a man of his class and station should aspire to. Little
wonder, too, that Joinville invariably praises Louis IX when the mon-
arch remains within the guidelines of *preudomie* and takes him to task
when he transgresses those guidelines. For in transgressing the bound-

aries of that ideal, even out of religious zeal, Louis IX is in fact pre-
varicating against himself, by falling short of the highest goal available
both to him and to his social class.

Joinville has no choice, therefore, but to condemn with his silence
any and all of the king's attempts to reduce the Christian faith to a
number of adolescent riddles. He can boldly tell Louis that his coldness
toward his wife is unbecoming to a man of sense and *preudomie* (116,
594). He can warn Louis sternly to beware his tendency to accept gifts
from persons asking favors of him and can advise him in affairs of the
world to "trust only those who knew most about them" (123, 628). Of
the king's alleged decision to brand the nose and lips of a Parisian burgher who had been found guilty of blasphemy, Joinville can only respond with the dry disclaimer: "I did not see it myself" (138, 685).
Of Louis's decision to embark on the last, fatal Eighth Crusade, Joinville can only remark that "those who advised him to go committed a
mortal sin" (144, 736). These are matters in which the king was guilty
either of excess or failure in matters of *preudomie,* a failure both to
himself and to his class.

It is with undisguised pride, on the other hand, that Joinville tells of
those occasions when the king acted like an unqualified *preudome.* Such
occasions far outnumber those when King Louis lapses into an unfortunate *beguinage.*[18] When he tells Joinville and Robert de Sorbon that a
man should dress according to his social degree (6, 38); when he refuses the demands of the bishops over matters of secular jurisdiction
(13); when he tells his sailors, on the way back from *outremer,* that
"there is perhaps no one on the ship who loves life any more than I
do" (133, 628); when he is willing to treat with the Saracens at Mansourah, even to the point of paying a huge ransom for his own life and
the lives of his men (71)—at moments like these King Louis is living
according to the code of *preudomie.*

With regard to the last instance, it is noteworthy to contrast the
king's attitude with that of Joinville's storekeeper, who proclaimed in
Egypt that "we should allow ourselves to be killed and thus we shall
go to Paradise."[19] While the Christian *preudome* will resort to all measures within reason to avoid martyrdom and prolong his life in the service of God and His Mother, only a *vilain* would be dimwitted enough
to provoke death in order prematurely to win paradise. Joinville
makes no attempt to conceal his feeling that such storekeepers are not
to be listened to.

The Christian ideal of Saint Louis, in short, was conditioned and
guided by the secular canons of his social class. The king's Christianity
was far closer to Joinville's than to the storekeeper's. Otherwise stated,

Joinville's sanctity is far closer to the king's than the seneschal has customarily been given credit for. Too long critics have spoken admiringly of the "foil" that Joinville provides for the holy king: "Joinville is human whereas the king is saintly, and together they make a harmonious pair," so the argument runs in simplified terms.[20] Joinville was quite as serious about his piety as the king. As a member of the feudal nobility he had the right to aspire to the heights of *preudomie;* and there is nothing in his text to justify the mere suggestion that he considered himself any less a Christian, any less an *exemplum,* any less a *preudome* than the king he served.

In his attitude toward the faith Joinville has sometimes been dismissed as a lovable buffoon, principally because he seemed bent on appearing like a man who takes his Christianity with Gallic moderation. Readers usually think of Joinville as the man "who would rather commit thirty mortal sins than be a leper"; who did not so much as lend an ear to his storekeeper who tried to make martyrdom sound attractive; who, at the point of being decapitated at Mansourah, did not feel that confession was necessary, "for I could not remember any sin I had committed" (70, 354); who while in a Saracen prison found the prospect of the afterlife far less invigorating than the good news that he was about to be released (66, 337); who confessed and absolved a fellow lord while in prison and then admitted to having forgotten everything the man had said (70, 355). Joinville, in short, often strikes his critics as a man who takes his faith with a measure of humanistic skepticism—a Montaigne before his time, as it were.

In this matter, as in several others, Joinville's allusions are perhaps more eloquent than his words. His highly personal commentary on the Nicean Creed is the work of a deeply reflective mind.[21] A man of little faith would perhaps not have shown Joinville's high courage at Acre, when a vast majority of the French lords, including the king himself, were tempted to return prematurely to France. A spiritual buffoon would surely not have erected a chapel in honor of Saint Louis after seeing him in a dream and have provided that chapel with an endowment that would allow a mass to be sung "for ever in his honour" (148, 767).

Joinville very probably took matters of faith with the utmost seriousness. His was neither the unrelieved dullness of the professionally devout nor the prissiness of the king himself, who once observed that the Christian's harshest curse-word, at the peak of a fit of temper, should not exceed "In truth it was so" (138, 686). He seemed unafraid of letting joy intrude on his piety; he was not alarmed that cheerfulness kept getting in the way. Nietzsche once remarked of Jesus that "his disciples should look more redeemed."[22] One imagines Joinville as looking redeemed. His book is a record not merely of one saintly life but of a collective attempt at *preudomie,* including his own. Of his stay at Acre he wrote: "Now I must tell you of the many hardships and tribulations I suffered at Acre, from which God, in whom I trusted as I trust in Him now, delivered me. I shall have these written down that those who hear them may also put their trust in God when they suffer hardship and sorrow, and so God will help them as He helped me" (80, 406).

In Caesarea, Joinville regulated his days and nights with the same liturgical devotion as the king. He had with him in his tent two chaplains who recited hours for him, "one of them saying Mass for me as soon as the dawn appeared, the other waiting until my own knights and those of my division had risen. . . . My bed was so placed in my tent that no one could enter without seeing me in bed; this I did to avoid any scandal about women" (98, 501–502). Such, thought Joinville, is the responsibility of the lord and *preudome.* Without ever explicitly saying so, he interpreted his station in life, his personal and social vocation, as a call to bear the French nobleman's burden: to provide a religious model, to achieve *preudomie.*

The *History of Saint Louis* is a tribute to those saints and martyrs who accompanied Louis IX on the Seventh Crusade. Of them the king was certainly the best known, but he was not the only saint or the only martyr. Neither, so far as one can be sure, was he the most saintly of the martyrs. The king's style of sanctity, though communicable and highly personal, was neither the only nor necessarily the best. As members of the same peerage the king and the lords were equals. Each of them was entitled to his own style, each might serve as a model for others to imitate. The king is not exclusively worthy of imitation, and the possibilities of patterning one's life after his (if Joinville is to be taken at his word in the following passage) seem curiously restricted to members of the king's own family: "Great will be the honour to all those of his house who strive to resemble him in well doing, and . . . great reproach . . . to those of his house who seek to do ill, for fingers will be pointed at them and it will be said that the holy king from whom they are sprung would have scorned to do such wrong" (143, 761).

Joinville's intention was not to hold up the figure of Saint Louis for the Christian's imitation, but to write a manual of *preudomie* in which the king figures as one of two principal illustrations. The reader may identify more easily with the king; or with Joinville; or he may even choose to admire "all those who served as pilgrims and crusaders" with the king in Egypt and Palestine. Whatever the individual response, the *History of Saint Louis* is fundamentally a book about a class and an institution rather than about a man, a book written "that those who hear it may have full confidence in that part of it which is the very truth I saw and heard myself" (149, 768).

The subject of the book was *preudomie*. Insofar as the king lived by the code, he was doing no more than abiding by the canons prescribed for a member of his class. To the degree he lived by these canons the king was worthy of praise; inasmuch as he occasionally broke these humane canons with his excessive zeal, he was to be reprimanded, albeit posthumously. Such was the way Joinville might, in his old age, have justified his book to members of his family or peerage. But his reservations being expressed, Joinville ends his book on a conciliatory note. His last ghostly encounter with the king takes place in a dream, and it reads like a reunion between two members of the same peer group who immediately strike a common chord and a common language: "Now I must tell you some things about St. Louis which will be to his honour, and which I saw in my sleep. It seemed to me, then, in my dream, that I saw him in front of my chapel at Joinville, and he was, I thought, wonderfully gay and light of heart; and I, too, was happy to see him in my castle, and said to him, 'Sir, when you leave, I will entertain you in a house I have in a village of mine called Chevillon.' He answered me with a laugh, 'My Lord of Joinville, by the faith I owe you, I have no wish to leave this place so soon' " (148, 766).

The *History of Saint Louis* can be abstracted from its time and read as a revealing biography of two of the most engaging figures in thirteenth-century France. It can also be considered in its own right as a treatise on kingship wherein the figure of a great prince is held up for the admiration and the imitation of posterity. In both regards Joinville's chronicle is being read as a traditional piece of medeval historiography perpetuating the Graeco-Roman idea that history is above all a narration of the acts and deeds of great men for the purpose of moral edification.

We have attempted to consider the *History* not according to this timeless or traditional point of view, but as a product of the mental equipment of the thirteenth century. For one cannot disregard the intellectual structures of the period in which Joinville lived. Although he never engaged in the dialectical debates of the schools, Joinville was convinced, like most of his contemporaries, that there is a structural bond between a concept and its concrete representations. A concept like *preudomie* has real existence, both in its individual representations and, ultimately, in the mind of God. In that regard, the concept, the idea, the institution is both nobler and more real, in the order of being, than even the most authentic of its concrete representations.

Joinville's book might thus be read as the description of the dynamic structural relationship between a universal and a singular. There are moments when the singular lives up to the requirements of the universal; there are moments when it falls short. But the structural bond between them is a real one. By Froissart's time, the mid-fourteenth century, that bond has broken entirely.

4   FROISSART: HISTORY
AS SURFACE

Born at Valenciennes in 1337, Froissart studied for the priesthood and received minor orders.[1] In 1356, he sailed to England where his compatriot, Queen Philippa of Hainaut, the wife of King Edward III, received him and took him into her service. While in the queen's employ the young cleric visited Scotland, France, and Italy. After the death of his patroness in 1369, Froissart completed his studies for the priesthood. He was given a parish near Mons in 1373. During the next decade, he often traveled to the court of Duke Wenceslas of Luxemburg at Brussels. In 1384, he became chaplain to Count Guy de Blois, and while continuing to occupy a canonry at Chimay, he often resided at the count's castle at Beaumont. During the last two decades of his life, Froissart continued to travel and enjoy courtly feasts. He returned several times to France and the Low Countries; in 1388, at the invitation of Count Gaston de Foix, he left for Béarn, gathering en route all the visual and oral information he could muster, especially on events in southwestern France and Spain. He went to England a last time in 1394 to visit the court of King Richard II. He was still alive in 1404. The exact year of his death is unknown.

Froissart's principal claim to literary immortality rests upon his *Chronicles of France, England, and Neighboring Countries,* an account in four books of events, principally the "hauts faits d'armes," which occurred in Europe between the accession of Edward II to the English throne (1307) and the death of Richard II (1400).[2] He began writing his narrative in 1370–71, at the request of Robert de Namur. His account of the years 1327–61 is largely a *réchauffé* of the chronicle of Jean le Bel, canon of Liège. The chronicle of the ensuing years (1361–

1400), however, is the product of extensive travel, direct experience, and personal interrogation of witnesses. Froissart reaches the heights of "grand reportage" with his account (in Book III) of the trip to Orthez in 1388. His alleged purpose was to accept an invitation sent him by Count Gaston de Foix and to gather a dossier of facts on the wars in Spain and in southwestern France at the time. Book III is curiously modern in that it is essentially a book about the genesis of a book. Froissart encounters a knight called Espaing de Lyon on his way to Orthez, and riddles him with persistent questioning until their arrival at the court of Count Gaston de Foix. At Orthez he releases this acquiescent victim, only to ply other members of the court with pertinent interrogations.

Although his project was ambitious, Froissart remained a perfectionist. He wrote at least four different versions of Book I and two versions of Book II. Books III and IV, which were completed in 1390 and 1398 (or 1400), respectively, exist in only one version.

He was a talented *raconteur,* and some of his scenes are among the most visually poignant in European literature; yet he is said to "lack a critical sense."[3] The ensuing pages are an attempt to measure the limitations of his visual and critical language so as better to comprehend his enthusiastic vision of the events of his time—the vision of a somewhat snobbish bourgeois cleric and courtier who happened to be an optical egalitarian.

Froissart is perhaps not the best traveled of the chroniclers, but he is the only one to allow his reader to feel the configuration of the terrain. A perusal of the *Chronicles* conveys a physical, almost giddying sensation of vastness in time and space: Froissart's stage stretches from the Hebrides to North Africa, from Portugal to the Rhine; his drama in four acts begins with the accession of Edward II (1307) and closes with the death of Richard II (1400); and though the author arrived on stage thirty years after the pageant had begun he gives the impression of having lived through it all.[4]

Villehardouin and Joinville perceive many of their scenes from the deck of a ship. Froissart shoots either on horseback or standing on solid ground. Villehardouin's chronicle, like Joinville's, is filled with lacunae during which time and space are either compressed or disproportionate to each other. It takes Joinville but a page to carry his reader from the southern coast of France to Cyprus, and Villehardouin takes a little more than a page to cover the waters between Corfu and the sea of Marmara.[5] Both chroniclers, like inexperienced sailors, lose their sense of time while at sea; and while covering several thousand nautical miles, they continue to record as if they had hardly moved. Their sea logs are singularly uneventful; motion seems to start up again only when they have reached solid ground, which measures it best. Their watches run best on land.

But Froissart, the most landgoing of the chroniclers, never seems to lose his sense of time. How caressingly aware he is of every inch of ground he covers! How conscious he is of the discreteness of objects upon a surface. "Tarbes is a large, beautiful city, seated on a plain among lovely vineyards. It is composed of outskirts, an inner city, and a castle, each enclosed within gates, walls, and towers, each separate from the other. The lovely river Lys, whose source is between the mountains of Béarn and Catelonia, flows into the city, cutting it in half."[6]

Such is Froissart's first topographical axiom: a given locus cannot be occupied by more than one object at a time. From this axiom, however elementary, derive the foundations of economic individualism and political atomism: "I noticed handsome castles and fortresses on both sides of the river. Those situated on the far side, to our left, belonged to the Count of Foix, and those on our side to the Count of Armagnac."[7] From it derive military and physical laws. A severe limitation of space can be a crucial military factor, like the narrow passage at Mont-Pezat, a Pyreneean Thermopylae.[8] In a remarkably Flaubertian passage, Froissart describes a crowd forcing its way into a room of the royal palace in Paris in order to watch a spectacle. The spectators suddenly, unexpectedly, find themselves colliding like molecules of vapor in a heated container:

> In the center of the palace there had been built an artificial wooden castle, forty feet high, twenty long, and twenty wide, with towers on each corner, and a much higher tower in the middle. The castle was supposed to represent Troy the Great, and the tower in the center was the palace of Ilion. The arms of the Trojan warriors, like those of King Priam, his brave son Hector, his other children, and other kings and princes, were emblazoned on flags. . . . [The Trojans and Greek fight a simulated battle.] The games, however, did not last very long because of the great crowd of spectators looking on. In the heat and pressure [presse] of the crowd, some began to feel most uncomfortable. On the side of the room near the door of the parliament, where a good number of ladies and damsels were sitting, a table was toppled over. The swelling of the crowd and the intense heat of the room suddenly forced the ladies and the damsels to rise to their feet. The queen (Isabella of Bavaria) began to feel ill. Someone had to smash a window behind her in order to let in some air.[9]

So physical is Froissart's sense of space that his description of a movement over a surface takes roughly the same time to read as it would take to cover the surface on foot. Froissart's sense of time is either commensurate with distance covered or implicitly referred to as a measurable quantity. An especially striking instance of this commensurability is Isabella of Bavaria's arrival at the gates of Paris, where she is to marry Charles VI in 1389. On the first day of the festivities, the queen and her train of ladies are carried on litters from the Gate of Saint Denis to the cathedral of Notre Dame, and from there to the royal palace (located on the present site of the Palace of Justice). The events of that first day, which take several pages to relate, last from Sunday morning at sunrise ("à heure de relevée") until late in the evening. The queen and her train stop many times during the procession. The processional route is lined with thousands of spectators and decorated with floats, flowers, and fountains gushing forth wine. The queen stops several times to listen to children's choirs or to watch mock reenactments of great historical events (e.g., Richard of England's crusade against the Saracens). Froissart remarks that this spectacle lasted "a good space [of time]" ("dura une bonne espace"), as if to comment on both its length and its size.[10] The description of the procession from the Saint Denis gate to the royal palace reads as if one were covering the distance on foot.

Froissart's recording of visual impressions unrolls with a regularity which one might best liken to a sequential, panoramic "take." During the procession from the Saint Denis gate to Notre Dame cathedral, there is always a smooth transition from one object to the other along the route, each transition marked syntactically by conjunctions such as "et puis" and "après." Sometimes the chronicler turns his eye away from the people and the decorations lining Saint Denis Street and points it downstreet toward the cathedral. The reader is then allowed a long-range view of the remainder of the route, as far as the Notre Dame bridge: "Then the lords and ladies saw, to their right, in front of the chapel of Saint Jacques a lavishly decorated stage, wholly covered with high-warp tapestry. . . . On both sides of Saint Denis Street as far as the Chatelet, even as far as the great bridge [the actual Pont Notre Dame], each house was covered with high-warp tapestry illustrating various historical events. It was truly a pleasurable sight to behold."[11]

The great ball at the court of Charles VI is also recorded cinematically. During this sequence, the chronicler's eye follows the action at every instant: as the king and his five companions put on their disguises in an adjoining room; as the king, after reviewing the fire hazards with one of his companions, sends a footman into the ballroom to order each of the torchbearers to stand near the walls and not to approach the dancers until they have finished their dance; as the duke of Orléans, unaware of the king's order and of the performance about to take place, enters the ballroom with four knights and six torchbearers and begins to dance; as the six "savages" enter in Indian file (with the king at the tail end), disguised in a resinated linen cloth; as the king detaches himself from the file in order to tease the duchess of Berry, who fails to recognize him; as the duke of Orléans draws near the dancers with one of his torchbearers in order to identify them; as the five "savages" are set afire like human torches, one of them saving his life by jumping into a large vat of dishwater; as the queen faints; as the king leaves the room to change his clothes; as bedlam and panic overtake the room.[12] So uninterruptedly does Froissart's eye record the scene that one might imagine its historical length as roughly commensurate with the length of the narrative.

Again, in Book III, Froissart's narrative measures a distance as it unfolds. During the voyage to Béarn, Espaing de Lyon's anecdotes line the narrative as if to while away the time between one town and another; and Froissart is always the one to interrupt his interlocutor so as to remind him and the reader that during all this time they have been drawing closer to their destination: "The stories Sir Espaing de Lyon was telling me were both very pleasant and relaxing. The road seemed much shorter as a result" ("Et m'en sembloit le chemin trop plus bref").[13]

Froissart, like the rest of his readers, assumes that there is a link both real and linguistic between time and travel. One speaks of "lengths" of time; both time and distance are referred to as "long" or "short." Why this automatic coupling of two distinct notions? The measuring of time, after all, need not be linked to travel, but surely, one's consciousness of time passing is best related with displacement over a surface. One is better aware of the passing of time while in a train or car than while one is immobile or inactive. It seems easier to be aware of the passing of time if it measures a distance traveled than if it does not, as it is retrospectively easier to reconstruct the activities of a week of travel than those of a week spent idly at home.

Can Froissart's flair for reconstructing the continuity of events not be related to his constant travels on the road where cinematic sequences are easier to recall. In his chronicle, *illic* and *tunc* are nearly always the inseparable factors of the same event. He often associates the moment of an event, even a banal interior occurrence such as a recollection or a sudden notion, with the place where it occurred: "While he was recounting these adventures, we passed the Pas au Larre and the castle of Marcheras, where the battle had taken place, and we approached the handsome and well-fortified castle of Barbesan, situated at about a league from Tarbes. . . . He [Espaing de Lyon] showed me the castle and town of Montgaillard across the river and the road that leads directly to Lourdes. At that moment it occurred to me to ask the knight how the duke of Anjou had behaved when the castle of Mauvoisin had surrendered to him."[14]

One is impressed by Froissart's realistic descriptions of events he experienced at second hand. Had he not been scrupulous by habit in distinguishing events he witnessed directly from those he reconstructed from hearsay, the reader could never tell one from the other. He has an extraordinary capacity for visualizing imaginary scenes in space. When he describes things he has not seen he seems especially interested in reconstructing full-scale models with known units of measurement rather than in determining cause, consequence, or significance. In describing an expedition to the Barbary Coast, led by the duke of Bourbon in 1390, he remains exasperatingly vague about the reasons for the expedition and its results; but he does inform the reader about the units of measurement he used to reconstruct the action: "I, John Froissart, author of these *Chronicles,* have never been to Africa. . . . In order to describe it more precisely, I inquired about means, manner, and size. Since I had often been to Calais in my lifetime, those of my informants who knew that town used it as their reference as approximately as they could. They told me that the African city is shaped like a bow, as is Calais, with the curve facing the sea."[15]

When he describes a situation Froissart is more aware than other chroniclers of the surface on which they are displayed: "This African city . . . was extremely well built, and surrounded with high walls and towers. At the mouth of the harbor, in front of the town, there stood a tower higher than all the others. . . . The walls of the town, seen from the Christians' side, were entirely covered and decorated with tapestries, resembling bed-coverings on every side, as far as the eye could see. . . . The night the Christian fleet approached the town, it remained at the entrance of the harbor, about a league out to sea."[16]

Froissart's portrait of Count Gaston de Foix is difficult to picture at first: "At the time I was his guest, Count Gaston de Foix was about fifty-nine years old. I have known many knights, kings, princes, and other lords in my time; but I have never seen anyone so handsome and well built as he was. He had a flushed, jovial face. His bright, gray eyes fell affectionately on whatever he pleased to look at. He was so perfect in every way that excessive praise of him is impossible. He liked and disliked what he felt he should like and dislike. He was intelligent, authoritative, wise in giving counsel."[17] The picture gradually comes into focus as the places where habitual actions occur are related in more specific detail: "Every day he recited nocturns in his private chamber . . . and had alms distributed at his door. . . . Sometimes (but not every day), he would take money from some of the coffers in his chamber to help a knight or squire who happened to be staying at his court ["pardevers luy"]. . . . He had four secretaries to write and recopy his letters. When he came out of his private chamber, they had better be ready!"[18]

From this series of localized "shots" of the count, the chronicler changes to a more dynamic description of his subject in motion:

> The Count, then, lived in the manner I have just described. And when he came out of his chamber at midnight to have supper in his hall, he was always preceded by twelve valets, each carrying a lighted torch. The hall, brightly lighted by twelve torches held at the head of the count's table, was always filled with knights and squires. There were always many tables set for those who wished to have supper. No one was allowed to address the count at table unless he was called upon. He usually ate large quantities of fowl, especially the wings and legs. He drank sparingly. He enjoyed listening to minstrels' songs (being well versed in music), and made his clerks sing songs, rondos, and lays. He usually sat about two hours, looking pleased at the sight of the exotic dishes that were set before him, and had them distributed to the knights and squires at the other tables.[19]

Froissart's picturing of images on a surface, whether or not he has witnessed them directly, extends to states of consciousness as well. Whereas most literary artists convey complex, intricate states of consciousness together—Vergil uses but one line to convey Dido's mixed sense of pleasure, shame, apprehension, and melancholy (*Aeneid,* IV, 23)—Froissart seems to make it a point to dissect and juxtapose mental attitudes that occur together. Whether out of disinclination or lack of talent, Froissart is anything but an expert in describing states of soul. His only way of conveying simultaneous states of consciousness, however fused they may be in reality, is to place them side by side.

During Froissart's sojourn at Orthez, for example, an old squire vividly recalls the circumstances attending the death of the count's beloved fifteen-year-old son. The count of Foix, thinking his son wishes to poison him, has thrown the boy into a dungeon.[20] Broken in spirit by his father's unjust accusation, the young lad refuses his food and begins to let himself die of starvation. The guards beg the count to take pity on his son, who has not touched food since entering prison. The narrator then recalls that the count grew angry. The reader finds it hard to imagine how anger alone, unless joined with other emotions such as pity, tenderness, or impatience, would have impelled the count to visit the boy in his cell; and Froissart seems unable to describe the web of emotions—anger, repressed tenderness, pride, self-assertion, concern for the boy's health—triggering off the count's nervous, irrational gesture: he points his dagger at the boy's throat in order to "bring him to his senses" and accidentally pricks his jugular vein. Only when he learns that this seemingly innocuous gesture has made his already anemic son bleed to death does the count lapse into a Davidic display of grief. Throughout the scene, one discerns in the count's conduct a set of warring emotions, but Froissart limits his description of the count's mental states to a linear juxtaposition of anger and grief, well separated in time: "Upon hearing this [the news that his boy was not eating his food], the count grew angry. . . . Then [upon hearing of the boy's death], the count grew immeasurably sorrowful and began to lament for his son."[21]

Froissart again places mixed states of consciousness side by side when he recalls Pierre de Craon's reaction to the news that he has just been exiled from the court of King Charles VI: "That day Sir Pierre de Craon was told . . . that his services were no longer needed at the king's court and that he should look for another master. . . . When Pierre saw himself being fired in this manner, he was sorely ashamed; he took the news quite angrily and spitefully; he could not conceive or imagine why he was being fired, for he had never been warned; in fact he requested that the king and the duke of Touraine grant him an audience, but once again he was told that neither the king nor the duke wished to speak to him. When he realized that he was being ejected, he gathered his belongings and left Paris, very melancholic."[22]

Froissart orders Pierre's feelings in a linear sequence, their discreteness being emphasized by the paratactical construction of the sentence. One must imagine that Pierre's shame, anger, and spite burst simultaneously, while his need to know why he was being exiled and his request for an audience with the king followed in close succession. Froissart, however, juxtaposes the character's shame, his spiteful anger, his self-interrogation, his request for an audience, and his departure after being turned down almost as if they were successive objects disposed along a line at equidistant points.

Froissart's consciousness of space and spatial metaphor is perhaps nowhere more evident than in his account of the mental breakdown of King Charles VI.[23] That tragic event occurs while the king is traveling: Froissart was neither the first nor the last to associate exotic or destructive psychic experiences with travel through space. Though Froissart does not stress the symbolic nature of the place, it is pertinent to note that the location of the king's breakdown is a *selva oscura:* the forest of Le Mans. The accumulation of symptoms coincides with the progression of the king's train from the town into the forest. How symbolic is the appearance at the edge of the forest of that ragged old Tiresias, "plus fol que sage," who suddenly takes hold of the king's reins and cries, "King, do not go forward! Go back, for you have been betrayed!" How prophetic the fool's words turn out to be! The king's progression into the forest is indeed an advance toward self-betrayal, as if each of the symptoms were displayed like a milestone along the road, and as if each tree represented another step toward madness. "Le roy et sa routte passèrent oultre," Froissart comments of the fool's sudden appearance, his ambiguous verb suggesting that the king was determined both to disregard warning signs and to pursue his way.

In mid-forest, Charles VI begins to see imaginary enemies rushing upon him on the road: "et vint au roy en advision que grant foison de ses ennemis lui couroient sus pour l'occire."[24] His total collapse coincides with his illusion of being somewhere else on an imaginary battle field: "et cuida bien estre en une bataille."[25] His temporary recovery of sanity signals a symbolic return to the point of departure: "Il fault retourner au Mans." The search for a permanent cure is described as the need to discover a *locus amoenus* where the king might convalesce: "We must take counsel and look for an appropriate spot for him that he might recover his health as soon as possible."[26]

Froissart's investigations as a reporter can be described as a progression in space and time. Nowhere is such a progression more obvious than during his voyage to Orthez. Each day marks a step forward, not only in time and space, but in discovery, particularly the days spent with Sir Espaing de Lyon, that equestrian treasure trove of pertinent information: "I was quite pleased by the anecdotes Sir Espaing de Lyon told me. I listened to them with great pleasure and retained them perfectly. On the road we were traveling together; whenever we stopped in a hostel, I would jot his stories down, whether it was evening or morning, so that I might better remember them in times to come. Writing by hand is the most retentive of memories."[27] What, after all, is *écriture,* if not the ordering of thought or feeling on a surface, the spacing of elements which have neither order nor place, capturing that elusive essence which, in Montaigne's words, "extravaguait au vent"?[28]

Even the roving reporter's pursuit of answers has about it a progressive, linear quality. Each question goes a step beyond the information provided by the previous answer, leaning upon it like a sprinter toeing his mark. Each answer is a step forward, not toward the discovery of a general truth but toward the accumulation of particular, concrete details. Froissart's questions are a steady, horizontal march forward. He pursues his informants like a hunter after game. When, in the course of their ramblings, Sir Espaing tells him that Count Gaston de Foix has murdered Pierre Ernault, his reporter's instincts tell Froissart that the chase must now begin.

> "Ha! By Saint Mary," I said to the knight, "don't you think that was cruel?"—"Whatever it was," he answered, "that's the way it happened. He kept his first cousin, the Vicount of Chastelbon, his heir, eight months prisoner in the tower of Orthez; then he had him ransomed for forty thousand francs."—"What, Sir," I asked, "has the count of Foix no children? I've just heard you say that the Viscount of Chastelbon was his heir."—"In God's name," he replied, "he has no children by any legitimate wife; but he does have two young bastard sons, whom you shall soon be meeting: Sir Yvain and Sir Gratian. He loves them both as much as himself."—"Didn't he ever marry?"—"Yes, and he is still married; but Madame de Foix doesn't live with him."—"Where does she live?" I asked.—"In Navarre, for the king of Navarre is her cousin. She was the daughter of King Louis of Navarre."—"Didn't the count of Foix have any children by her?"— "He did: a handsome boy, who was most dear to his father and the people. . . ."—"And, Sir, what became of this boy? Can you tell me?"—"I can," he answered, "but not now. The story is too long."[29]

Froissart's questions have led him over a winding path to the threshold of a closed, forbidden castle. One almost hears the rising alarm, the progressive quickening of breath, in the questioner's voice as he forges on. His final question is almost a cry of dread and exhaustion, as if the reporter were fatigued by his inquiry and regretted having embarked upon such a labyrinthine adventure.[30]

Froissart remarks in one of his Prologues: "Every edifice is built and cemented stone upon stone, and great rivers are made up of many streams and fountains. So, too, science is a compilation made by many clerics, each unaware of what the other knows."[31] Thus Froissart must resort to a spatial metaphor to clarify his conception of the chronicler's work. The *Chronicles* themselves he considers a composite of constituent blocks. The end product is not qualitatively different from the component parts. His sentences like his paragraphs are not a synthesis but an accumulation of independent parts. If he uses the coordinate conjunction *et* so often it is because he is accustomed to thinking analytically rather than synthetically. His most frequently used coordinating conjunction is as indispensable to his craft as cement to a mason's. Froissart needs plenty of conceptual space in order to write.

Whether describing exterior action or inner consciousness he is that type of writer of whom Pascal would have said: "One thought alone occupies his mind; he cannot think of two things at the same time." His constant use of coordinately connected sentences enables him to center each of the independent clauses about the telling of a single fact. More than any of the other chroniclers, Froissart must juxtapose his internal images in order better to see them, not in one another, but next to one another. He needs to project time into space.

Hence Froissart is hardly conscious of real time. None of the characters in the Chronicles, including the narrator himself, ever seems conscious of his internal duration. Nowhere is there a panoramic remembrance of things past or a vivid consciousness of the present gnawing away at the future. Those characters who finally do become aware of interior time are too late in doing so. The one perception of time is that of a time burned out, *usé*; and even during such moments of consciousness time appears like a retrospective space which one has more or less successfully filled up. "My Lord, thank God we have used up our time in peace and joy and prosperity," declares Queen Philippa to her husband on her deathbed: "nous avons en pais et en joie et en prospérité *usé nostre temps.*"[32] Froissart's characters seem to think of time only when it is past. Time, in Froissart's chronicle, is something fixed, determined, frozen in the snows of yesteryear, never a dynamic, ongoing force.

This might explain why Froissart's characters never seem to learn. Time brings an accumulation of "high feats of arms," never of wisdom; a dispersal of time and energy in action, rarely a ripening in time. Like comic characters (even though the incidents they experience are not at all humorous) they do not seem to profit from their mistakes. The reader is never allowed to get inside their skin or grasp them intuitively, even when they suffer. He must subjectify them, read into their character through their outside delineations. Froissart allows for no other response.

The reader is therefore provided with a series of projections of the character at a given moment in a given place. After observing a character in action a number of times in successive places, the reader might then form a composite image of that character by collating, in his mental scrapbook, his collection of snapshots. Froissart's characters can never be immediately apprehended as subjects. His gallery of images is insubstantial. One grasps those delineations which project themselves into space upon the reader's senses, but the internal, temporally progressive dimension of the characters is missing. One must assume it exists, as one imagines a third dimension in looking at a portrait or painting with an illusive spatial background. The chronicler's vision of the world, being external, is literally superficial.

Might it not therefore be nominalistic? It is a striking but hardly surprising detail of Froissart's life that it coincided with the height of the Ockamist movement. Although next to nothing is known of Froissart's education, it would be quite surprising if this well-traveled clerk had not managed to absorb a few Ockamist notions at one time or other in Flanders, France, or England. One is struck, in any case, by the irreducibly singular character of each historical event and by the chronicler's curious refusal to draw general inferences from so vast an experience. One would think that his endless gallery of personalities, his vast store of anecdotes, his wide travels would have awakened in him a need to compare, infer, abstract, or generalize. Yet his rare generalizations are deceptively banal. One senses in this sophisticate a regression to dubious words of wisdom whenever he begins to philosophize. "That's the way things go; those who have been harmed complain, and those who have profited rejoice."[33] "Now, there is nothing a man doesn't get tired of after a while."[34] "That is the way Fortune pays off her people: when she has raised them high on her wheel, she topples them over into the mud."[35] And so forth.

Froissart, of course, was no philosopher. The author of the *Espinette amoureuse* had more in common with court minstrels and Flemish painters than with a circle of scholastic disputants. His concentration on the singular event cannot, however, be laid exclusively to the charge of personal inclination. Does he not profess a loose, implicit conviction that universal ideas, contrary to singular events and objects, have no extra-mental reality and are therefore unworthy of the annalist's concern? Must the chronicler's language not adapt itself to the concrete singularity of reality itself? Rather than provide his reader with ideas, types, or essences, Froissart seems to consider his task as the recording (*enregistrement*) of series upon series of similar, even repetitive instances, leaving it to the reader to draw his own inferences. Let the reader create his own universals.

Froissart's implicit nominalism may explain why the *Chronicles,* spanning nearly a century in time, produce an over-all impression of ahistoricity. One perceives a series of instants, never time; a series of objects, never dynamic subjects; repetitive actions and events, never organic progression. The "faits d'armes" of 1390 are described in terms identical to those of 1350; any character sturdy enough to survive three or four decades of jousting and fighting is sure to have learned nothing from the experience. As to Froissart, four decades of travel and courtly feasting seem to have provided him with a rich store of incidents or anecdotes, but he seems none the wiser. He has been to many places; he still has no depth.

One begins to understand why Froissart has sometimes been criticized for his materialism.[36] Space being, according to some definitions, the "world of the homogeneous,"[37] one comprehends Froissart's apparent indifference to chivalric or moral values. Was the chivalric order as crass as he depicts it, or was he simply unable to take any ideal (i.e., universal) concept seriously? Might Froissart's materialism not be linked to his nominalistic distaste for abstraction, to his instinctive need to order all his singular representations?

One is impressed, at all events, by his reduction of chivalric morality to a game of numbers, risks, gambles, prices, prizes, and exchanges. Revenge in battle becomes a game of one-upmanship: if the enemy decapitates two hostages, one responds by decapitating three.[38] Life and death hang by the thread of a gratuitous gamble, such as King Charles the Sixth's sudden impulsion to race the duke of Touraine back to Paris from the Pyrenees.[39] The dividing line between a playful joust and a live battle is so fine that the reader can hardly distinguish one from the other.[40] The most admired figurants of the *Chronicles* are either well-established feudal lords like Gaston de Foix, who keeps "a great number of servants and prisoners"; or rags-to-riches actors like the opportunist Croquard who grew up as a penniless page boy, and "in a short time became so rich that he was said to have sixty thousand *écus,* not counting his horses, of which he had twenty or thirty in his stables"; or amiable cynics like Bascot de Mauléon, whose account of his past glories is heavily spiced with the words *bonne étrenne, trente mille francs, grand finances, grand profit, pactis, pillage,* and *fortune.*[41] Bascot's account of his rise to fortune, incidentally, concludes with the disarming admission that the only reason he has always fought on the side of the king of England is that "my inheritance is located in the region of Bordeaux."[42] For Bascot, as for so many of Froissart's characters, personal destiny depends on the locus of one's birth. In the beginning was the place.

Froissart, then, does quantify his values. As the best knight is the one who sustains the largest number of battles, sieges, prisoners, and prizes, so the best chronicler is the one who can boast the largest store of anecdotes, places traveled, people known.

To argue that Froissart's chronicle is a perfect mirror of the decline of chivalry in fourteenth-century France would be hasty. In any case, the image of the mirror seems inadequate. Rather than reflect the events of his time in a *speculum historiale,* Froissart's eye records the events of his time and cuts them up into measurable lengths; and it is curiously restricted to recording outer surface. It needs to project its representations not only of visual but of psychic phenomena into space. But such, perhaps, is the fate of any literary attempt to provide a highly visual and cinematic representation of a living, fluid reality. The reader's eye must intervene in order to pour life into a static mosaic of inert representations. Perhaps more than any other chronicler, Froissart needs a reader in order to bring his chronicle to life.

5 CHASTELLAIN AND LA MARCHE: HISTORY AS NARCISSISM

GEORGES CHASTELLAIN and Olivier de la Marche are the most outstanding of the historiographers who wrote while in the service of the Burgundian dukes, John the Fearless (1404–19), Philip the Good (1419–67), and Charles the Bold (1467–77).[1] Georges Chastellain (1405–75) studied at Louvain, traveled widely, and took part in the campaigns of King Charles VII against the English between 1435 and 1446. He was appointed squire to Duke Philip the Good that year and named official historiographer in 1455. His *Chronicle of the Dukes of Burgundy* is a "book containing all the great deeds of Christendom, especially those in this noble kingdom of France and its dependencies," from 1419 to 1474.

Chastellain's contemporaries considered him the greatest historian of his time. Olivier de la Marche, his official successor, envied "George the Adventurous" for his loftiness of thought and expression: "mon père en doctrine, mon maistre en science, . . . la perle et l'estoille de tous les historiographes." Historians of historical writing since the last century have echoed Olivier's naive praise, often in similar terms. Auguste Molinier considered Chastellain "the best representative of the Burgundian historical school, and . . . one of the most remarkable French writers of the fifteenth century." Joseph Calmette wrote that "Chastellain is not only a chronicler of the first order, without whom our knowledge of the fifteenth century would be truly very deficient; he is an authentic historian, let us say a French Thucydides among so many Herodotuses of more or less high quality who abound in our medieval historiography."

Olivier de la Marche (1425–1502), who envied Chastellain's "subtil parler" and Molinet's "rethoricque tant experte," spent his life in the shadow of the Burgundian dukes. A page boy during the reign of Philip the Good, he served successively as stable boy, squire, maître d'hôtel, ambassador, warrior, poet, and chronicler. He was an assiduous facto- tum whose loyalty to the duchy continued well after the death of Charles the Bold in 1477. He continued to serve Mary of Burgundy, Charles the Bold's only daughter, after her marriage to Maximilian of Austria in 1477. La Marche, whose *Memoirs* record nearly seventy years of con- temporary history (1435–1502), had neither Chastellain's "subtil par- ler" nor his fatuous notion of the "high" style. He seems to have been blessed with a measure of lucidity in appraising himself, a rare quality in the Burgundian court; and, unlike "le grand Georges," he was sensi- ble enough to submit the merry, whirling spectacle of Burgundian court life to the occasional scrutiny of his personal judgment. That experience was both vital and sobering: Olivier realized that the Burgundian pag- eant was doomed to collapse under the excessive weight of its own décor. His quiet lucidity endears him to some readers, and his historical talent seems quite as substantial as that of Chastellain.[2]

Some chroniclers are voyeurs, others exhibitionists. There are those who consider historiography as a profession akin to criminology: they spy through keyholes, peer curiously into private chambers, enlarging small and to all appearances insignificant images. Their eye is a small, magnifying lens that enables the reader to notice objects and events that might otherwise have remained invisible or gone unobserved. Exhibi- tionist chroniclers, on the other hand, consider it their business to dis- play already notorious events and in so doing to display themselves. Like the Lady in a famous tapestry, they hold up a mirror to their civi- lization, not unmindful that the quality and tone of the image depends largely upon the quality of the mirror.

During the reigns of the last Burgundian dukes, Philip the Good and Charles the Bold, historiographers were assumed to be official mirrors. One explanation for their presence was perhaps that the dukes enjoyed looking at themselves; and if, especially during the half-century that separates the accession of Duke Philip from the death of his son, there were an impressive number of court historians who looked upon their *oeuvre* as a "miroir et doctrine" of Burgundian civilization, they knew that the demand for flattering reflections was high and the price en- ticing. During the better part of the fifteenth century, history is as characteristically Burgundian as tapestry is characteristically Flemish. Around 1400 or so, "History became a Burgundian enterprise,"[3] and the most truly Burgundian of these historians, perhaps because they were so directly involved in the affairs of court, were Georges Chastellain and Olivier de la Marche.[4]

Like Froissart (whom they had read and admired), both came from Flanders and had inherited Sire John's visual curiosity, his talent for ordering his representations on a surface, his fascination for singular, colorful events, his distaste for introspection. There seems to be a distinctly Flemish predisposition to view reality in terms of texture and color. Even the most austere of Flemish painters, mystics, and humanists—a Ruysbroek, an Erasmus, a Van Eyck—cannot conceal their love of substance, flesh, and color. So it is with Chastellain and La Marche. Their ideas invariably are made flesh. They rarely dwell on passion, emotion, or internal conflict, and they seem to represent abstractions as visually as they can. La Marche spends well over a hundred pages describing the ten-day wedding celebration of Charles the Bold and Margaret of York, yet he rarely carries his private judgments beyond two or three lines. And when Chastellain defends himself against those who accuse him of having biased his chronicle in favor of the Burgundian dukes, he allegorizes and projects his conflict in a dialogue between the author and his psyche, significantly entitled *Exposition sur vérité mal prise*.

Inheritors of Froissart, both Chastellain and La Marche seem to concentrate upon visual representations. From the very outset they are bound to disappoint readers who approach them in the hope of discovering intuition, discernment, extrapolation, or criticism. Like the Canon of Chimay they seem to display their images to such an extent that space, playing a role analogous to that of the basic color in Flemish tapestries, serves as a frame for the insertion of the various pictures.

Chastellain and La Marche seem to have considered it their function to project the Burgundian image by reflecting it, but images can neither be reflected nor projected without first being acquired. The primordial historical activity is sight, as Chastellain suggests in the opening lines of his *Prologue*. From the beginning of time, men have seen and interpreted the events of their time in the light of religious or mythological systems. The succession of empires through history has made it clear that the historical spectacle is nothing but misery and vexation of spirit. The historian himself, his vision dimmed by darkness and the thick fogs of lamentation ("né en éclipse de ténèbres ès espesses bruynes de lamentation") has seen the glorious French kingdom conquered by the English, "devant mes yeux." He has seen honor driven out of royal palaces; truth, justice, and loyalty banished from the kingdom. Taking the larger view of the present calamity he will collate the information given him by his contemporaries with what he himself has seen and discovered ("veu et congneu").[5]

After recording his images, the historian must reproduce them. Of the death of Duke Philip the Good, Chastellain writes significantly that "now his visual imprint has entered me as it has all those who loved him. Now we shall enjoy his image as in a new mirror, a reflection of the first that has vanished."[6] In both a physical and a metaphorical sense, the chronicle must be a "new mirror" of those events which have made an imprint on the chronicler's imagination. The chronicle is both a reproduction of images fixed upon the mind's eye and a reflection wherein a society can admire itself. It is in a double sense a "nouvel miroir . . . image du premier esvanouy," a new mirror, an image of the original, which has vanished.

Sight, therefore, is both the means and the purpose of the chronicle. The chronicler sees and reproduces his vision so that his reader may see and take visual delight. In his *Exposition sur vérité mal prise,* Chastellain likens the chronicle to a "perpetual mirror" through which the reader acquires not merely spiritual delight, a lofty vision of man's ingenuity, but a "corrected" image of himself.[7] And in his *Prologue,* La Marche calls the "abridged memories" which he has resolved to commit to writing "a useful mirror and doctrine for times to come."[8] In another passage he describes his purpose as that of delighting his readers with live, visual representations of events which they have not witnessed directly.[9]

If Burgundian history is a mirror, then one must say of all its events that "così è si vi pare." Things are exactly what they seem. The chronicle is not an intuition of hidden essences but a representation of outer configurations ("pareure"). Essences may or may not exist, but it is not the business of the historian to deal with them. Chastellain's entire chronicle belies his passing suggestions that exterior events should be dealt with as summarily as possible, "since the vanity and pomp of this world are as a bottomless, boundless river."[10] It would of course be exaggerated to interpret Chastellain as thinking that essences have no objective reality except insofar as they are projected upon the eye of the beholder, but he is surely not interested in essences unless they do in fact so project themselves. In his portrait of Duke Philip the Good, for example, he is especially bent on showing that the duke's *pareure* gave a faithful outward account of the man's inner self. The duke's physical makeup seemed to fit the requirements of a Platonic model: he was of "average" height; his neck was "proportionate" to his body, his face was of "convenient" length; his mouth was symmetrical, "en juste compas." His face also seemed the spatial projection of an inner harmony: "His inner disposition appeared on his face; there was a correspondence between his morals and his physical makeup, an identity between the inner and the outer man. There was no contradiction between heart and face: both were in harmony with the man's nature. His face was that of a leader. His natural talents entitled him to the crown. Among the princes of this world he shone like a star. His eye seemed to proclaim, 'I am a prince.' "[11]

La Marche, like Chastellain, is more attentive to outer configuration than to essence. Despite his occasional recourse to cognitive verbs, he does not look upon his chronicle as a medium of conceptual knowledge; there is no slip of the pen when he describes the purpose of his chronicle not as a logical but as a visual demonstration ("monstrer et faire apparoir") of his patron's legitimacy.[12] How many times does Olivier say of an event, no matter how inherently tragic, "It was a beautiful sight to behold."[13] So conscious is he of apearance that history seems to be judged upon its esthetic merits alone: the funeral procession of a king who has died prematurely is to him "a lovely sight to behold"; the prospect of Burgundian noblemen having to shave their hair in imitation of their duke is "unfortunate for the image [*pareure*] of the Burgundian house."[14]

Olivier's frequent use of the word *pareure* cannot be attributed to poverty of expression. He is rarely found wanting when it comes to expressing shades of meaning. What the ubiquity of this word betrays is an obsessive concern with the impression the Burgundian house makes both upon itself and rival houses. There is a great deal of show in his chronicle. Tournaments, jousts, weddings, funerals are invariably performed in the presence of viewers, the most watchful and critical eye being that of the supreme arbiter, the duke himself, surrounded by a nobility so magnificently attired "that it was a beautiful sight to behold."[15]

Sensitivity to outward configuration is inseparable from interest in light and coloration. In a significant passage, Chastellain refers to description and depiction as the historian's complementary objectives.[16] Chastellain seems to have been endowed with an equal sensitivity to line and color, and he is most receptive to the *clarté* without which neither can be perceived. This "clair homme," he recalls of Duke Philip, always projected a "clarity in keeping with the occasion."[17]

Like an artist, Chastellain is attracted to painted images. A funeral procession in honor of Henry V of England shows the king's embalmed body covered with a leather pall on which has been painted his life-size image ("la fiction de son image . . . vestue réelement et paincte au vif"). His body is drawn by four horses, their harness painted with various coats of arms.[18] Charles VI of France is honored in much the same way: he is drawn by a funeral cart, covered with a gold and vermilion winding sheet on which his life-size portrait has been drawn.[19]

Less visually sensitive than his master but more tactile, La Marche appears to respond to the texture of objects rather than to their outline or color. Whereas a Chastellain portrait impresses the reader with the brightness of its lighting and the neatness of its lines, La Marche's descriptions convey a stereoscopic quality and a sensation of tactile density. To say that La Marche is indifferent to color would be overstating matters, but he does appear more sensitive to the crude cloth of things than to their surface qualities. In a characteristic description of the Order of the Golden Fleece in formal attire, he recalls that "the squires wore robes of black damask cloth and doublets of figured crimson satin decorated with figures. The knights and members of the duke's council had long robes of black velvet and doublets of crimson velvet; and the servants and valets of the house were all dressed in black and purple cloth and woolen doublets. My Lord [Duke Philip] had contributed so much silk and woolen cloth for this show that it had cost him more than forty thousand francs. It was quite lovely, of course, to see this procession of knights and gentlemen so handsomely dressed."[20]

Chastellain and La Marche subscribe to some fundamental axioms of historical writing: the mirror of history must reflect not essences but outer configurations; every historical event must be cast in an appropriate "clarté" in order to be mirrored. They differ slightly, however, as to their visual tastes. Chastellain considers "pareure" as a projection of bright colors, while La Marche seems less awed by painted exteriors but more sensitive to tactile sensations and underlying substances. In keeping with his hero, Duke Philip the Good, Chastellain enjoys the glitter of objects but not the handling of them—"de son amas ne voult . . . n'argent manier, n'en sçavoir nombre"[21]—while La Marche, the faithful bursar, is indifferent neither to the texture nor to the cost of damask, silk, or wool.

While holding the mirror to their civilization, the Burgundian chroniclers had an opportunity to admire themselves. The Lady of the tapestry holds the mirror up to the Unicorn, but she also seems to be admiring herself in the Unicorn's self-satisfaction. So too with Chastellain and La Marche. Theirs was a self-conscious literary style reflecting a self-conscious culture; it made for a mutual self-propagating game of mirrors. Like Narcissus in a house of mirrors, Chastellain and La Marche had the capacity both to admire themselves in a mirror of their own creation and to reflect a civilization in the act of admiring itself. The Burgundian house was such a house of mirrors. The dukes were imbued with their own self-importance, highly encouraged in this pursuit by chroniclers who were habitually measuring them against their greatest forebears. Duke Philip, in Chastellain's own words, was "France's most magnificent prince since Charlemagne. . . . None of the Roman emperors, even the best among them, had ever been surrounded with as much ceremony, honor, and reverence as he was."[22] As he steps into his father's shoes, Charles the Bold is reminded that he is the "son of the most renowned duke the world has seen in a thousand years."[23]

Even if nature and custom had not been enough to make the dukes aware of their self-importance, their historiographers would still have managed to maintain them in a state of hypnotic narcissism. Chastellain would never have allowed Duke Philip to forget that he was competing in the eyes of history with the monarchs of the Old Testament, the Roman emperors, the Merovingian, Carolingian, and Capetian dynasties, not to omit his own Valois ancestors. The gauntlet of heroism he was constantly summoned to take up had been fashioned in great battles of the past by Saul or Solomon, Augustus or Titus. The impressive historical erudition of a Chastellain or a La Marche compelled the dukes constantly to measure themselves against the heroes of a Sallust, a Livy, or a Book of Kings.[24]

The greatest challenge to the dukes' self-evaluation, however, came from the centuries immediately previous to theirs. How did they compare with the *preudomes* of Joinville's time? Was it still possible for a fifteenth-century Burgundian duke to be a crusader? Was it feasible to rescue the holy places from the Infidel? Surely there was no dearth of opportunities for heroism or chivalric devotion. Henry V's most bitter regret, voiced at the time of his premature death in 1422, was that he had been unable to lead a crusade for the liberation of Jerusalem.[25] As early as 1442 the Byzantine emperor had sent Duke Philip the Good a request for men and warships to resist the Grand Turk.[26] The duke's reaction had been curiously narcissistic: he tilted with phantoms of his own creation, mistaking them for Saracens. His creation of the Order of the Golden Fleece, in 1429, had preceded the fall of Constantinople by twenty-four years; it came, however, at a time when the Turks were beginning to pose a threat to the existence of the city, and it might be considered Duke Philip's vicarious reenactment of the exploits he would have wished to perform in Turkish territory.

The Order of the Golden Fleece may have been the most outstanding instance of substitute heroism during Philip's reign. Philip would have liked, a modern Jason, to lead his Burgundian Argonauts to the rescue of the Christian empire in the East, but he seems to have contented himself, especially after 1435, with a surrogate derring-do. Perhaps the

most heroic events of his reign, after he had succeeded in consolidating
his power, are its convivial *entremets,* those theatrical, botanical, and
gastronomical reenactments of former chivalric exploits, which were
intended to stay the impatience of the dukes' dinner guests between
courses. The Burgundian fear of and fascination with *preudomie* seemed
best translated by scissors-and-paste reconstructions of the Golden
Fleece adventure or floral representations of crusading armies storming
the walls of Jerusalem. If the "Narcissus complex" can be described as
an inability to view the world as anything other than a subjective projection, then perhaps no event better suggests the existence of such
a complex at the Burgundian court after 1450 than La Marche's
memorable description of the "Pheasant's Banquet," held February 17,
1454.

La Marche devotes the better part of his fifty-page account to a description of the *entremets* that were performed during that banquet.[27]
The most pathetic (*pitoyable*) of these tableaux is an allegorical dramatization of the Church calling the Order to its aid. A Saracen giant, in
striped green attire, enters the banquet hall, leading an elephant on
whose back stands a miniature castle. In the castle sits a Lady (the
Church) dressed in white silk, who laments her captivity and begs her
listeners to "put an end to their life of ease." Now that the knights are
supposedly worked up to a feverish pitch of shame and indignation,
another symbolic character calling himself "Golden Fleece" enters the
banquet hall and presents the duke with a pheasant. He explains that
"at all great feasts and noble gatherings one offers the princes, lords,
and nobles a peacock or some other noble bird for making useful and
valid vows."

At that moment, Duke Philip, "who had planned this banquet with
a purpose in mind," pulls from his inside pocket a written text, which
he ostentatiously hands over to "Golden Fleece." It is a vow to deliver
the holy places. The Lady on the elephant, sensing that her salvation
is nigh, rejoices.[28]

Moved to tears of pity and compassion, the other nobles then commit their vows to writing; but they are careful to shade their heroic
promises with reservations and conditions. The duke comes forward
first and vows

> to God, to the Virgin Mary, His Mother, to the ladies present and to
> the Pheasant that, if it please our most Christian and victorious king
> [Charles VII] to take the cross, expose himself to danger for the de-
> fense of the Christian faith, and resist the damnable aggression of the
> Turk and his Infidels, provided I am in good health, I shall personally

serve him with my utmost strength in this holy crusade, so help me
God. If my lord the king's business does not allow him to leave, and
if he chooses to place another prince of his family or some other lord
at the head of his army, I promise to obey and serve his delegate. If
a sufficient number of other Christian princes are willing to sail, I
shall accompany them and assist them in defending the Christian faith
as best I can, provided my lord the king grants me his leave, and provided this dukedom, which I govern by the will of heaven, is peaceful
and secure. Such is my purpose and my duty: to let God and the
world know that, if the crusade fails, it is not, nor will it be, my fault.
If, finally, I receive word during the crusade that the Grand Turk
wishes to engage in single combat, I shall fight him, with the help of
almighty God and the Virgin Mary, whose help I always invoke.[29]

Each of the nobles then takes his turn in pronouncing a carefully
phrased vow, composed of a series of "if . . . then" propositions, the
validity of which hangs entirely upon the performance of an initial condition: "If the king wishes to take the cross." But as these vows are
being uttered, Charles VII, an ex officio member of the Order, is engaged in a full-scale war with the English in Normandy and Guyenne,
and no one seriously expects him to organize a crusade in the near
future nor to pronounce a vow to that effect.

The Pheasant's Banquet, then, is a magnificent illustration of verbal
fantasy posing as action. It seems to feature a doubly vicarious heroism
(or a heroism twice removed from the field of action) in that its par-
ticipants take the added precaution of stipulating that if, *per impossibile,*
the crusade were to take place, and if compelling reasons forced them
not to participate, then their presence in battle might be assured by one
or several paid replacements: "in case of illness . . . I shall send eight
or ten gentlemen who will be paid for a year."[30]

To be useful and valid each vow must be uttered in the presence of
a peacock, "or some other noble bird." One might gloss at length on the
symbolism involved in such a ritual, an immediate exegetical remark
being that peacocks and pheasants are traditionally considered symbols
of vanity and exhibitionism. Even the knights of the Order seem dimly
aware of the theatrical fatuousness of their words and gestures; the
pheasant is merely a surrogate mirror, and the entire Pheasant's Banquet is little more than a narcissistic orgy. The heroism of the Burgundian court is more picaresque than chivalric.[31]

The vows pronounced at the banquet, finally, have a magical character about them: words are uttered, however conditionally, as if they
could ipso facto be translated into deeds. The Burgundian court seems
to have wanted to blur the distinction between the conditional and the

indicative mood. Duke Philip's historic utterance, "I could have been king of France, had I wished," seems to have amounted to saying, "As duke of Burgundy, I am king, or better." The Burgundian word was a surrogate deed, providing both a sense of accomplishment and an excuse for inactivity, especially when the activity being considered served no political gain. One measures the height from which the thirteenth-century ideal of *preudomie* has fallen when one recalls King Louis's remark to Joinville that heretics are to be refuted not with subtle arguments but with a deep sword-thrust through the belly.

It has been suggested that the Burgundian chroniclers were themselves guilty of the narcissism which they reflect. Both Chastellain and La Marche are annoyingly obsequious; like nervous actors at curtain time, they stuff their prologues with wordy professions of incompetence for a task which, in any case, is already finished. After writing what is perhaps the most style-conscious and euphuistic of medieval historiographies, Chastellain prefaces his work by calling himself an "unworthy historiographer," "the least significant" of his profession. His most clinging obsession in the general prologue to his chronicle of the dukes of Burgundy is that of being judged partial, therefore unworthy, by his future readers. In his *Exposition sur vérité mal prise,* he defends himself against fictitious accusers of his own making (Indignation, Accusation, Vindication, and Reprobation), and in a fit of perverse narcissism he makes Dame Reprobation call him "a miserable cipher, a lowly earthworm, a wretch devoid of literary calling, talent, or intelligence, . . . a brainless, outrageous man."[32]

La Marche, too, uses tactics like preventive modesty and "captatio benevolentiae" when, in the prologue to his *Memoirs,* he describes himself to his patron Philip of Hapsburg as "a layman, not a clerk, of light intelligence and rough language," and regrets being shorn of the "style and subtle talk" of a Chastellain or a Molinet.[33] He writes with consummate insincerity that "I do not expect my small, ill-attired labor to be numbered among the chronicles written by the great minds of my time."[34] La Marche's modesty, however, rings truer than Chastellain's; his chronicle is refreshingly free of the "moi haïssable," whereas in Chastellain's chronicle of Duke Philip it is a ubiquitous presence whose concern for present and posthumous literary fame is transparent at every page.

One feels this concern for glory in the very sound of Chastellain's voice. He need not be taken literally when he requests his future readers "if ever they are curious enough to pay my works a visit . . . to pay no heed to the sound of my voice."[35] Such a studied use of preterition is of itself a sign that Chastellain is more conscious of the sound

of his voice than he admits; in fact no medieval French chronicler before him has ever been more aware of the parental link between rhetoric
and history. Perhaps no European historian since the late Empire had
made such extensive use of the spoken word, particularly the Thucy-
didean technique of recreating highly literary speeches without regard
to their historical likelihood. When the bishop of Tournay is sent to the
young Duke Philip to tell him that his father, Duke John the Fearless,
has been murdered at the bridge of Montereau, in 1419, the exordium
of his speech—in Chastellain's version—takes more than one-hundred-
eighty lines. Philip's mother, Duchess Michèle, responds with a lamentation of one-hundred-ten lines, consisting mostly of interjections and
ending with the words, "Woe is me, frail creature, woe, alas, woe, woe!"
Meanwhile the young duke, "having overcome his first wave of grief,"
opens the floodgates of "his second mourning" with "a bitter drainage
of words appropriate to his passion." Had he not wept, Chastellain
warns, I should have felt compelled to call him "bastard de toute vertu."
Philip's lament lasts one-hundred-twenty lines.[36]

Few writers are better aware than Chastellain of the galvanic effects
produced by the human voice. King Henry V of England speaks "with
a voice that cuts like razors . . . in grave tones, like a king."[37] One
of the reasons for Duke Philip's political success throughout his reign
is his perfect control of speech. He "looked at people when he spoke
to them and seemed to speak even when he was only looking at them.
He never spoke without reason and never paused for a word. He spoke
in moderate tones and never raised his voice even when he was angry.
. . . He never swore, was never profane or injurious, spoke favorably
of good people and compassionately of evil. I believe he never told a
lie. His mouth was his best seal, his word his best credential."[38] At
Ghent at the moment of assuming his murdered father's dukedom, Philip
addresses the Flemish nobles "in a lively voice; and although the matter
of his discourse was sad, yet he knew what terms and tones were necessary in order to convince them. No one failed to lend an ear or give the
speaker his undivided attention."[39]

The Burgundian chroniclers—especially Chastellain and La Marche
—wrote for both eye and ear. The Burgundian dukes made it a habit
to listen to the literature that was being written under their patronage.
La Marche remarks that Philip the Good "never retired without being
read for a couple of hours, and the lord of Humbercourt often read to
him, for he read and sustained one's attention well." The anonymous
translator of the *Chronicles of Pisa* records that Charles the Bold,
though he had little taste for studiousness, was always quite willing to
set some time aside for being read to.[40]

It is not certain whether or not parts of Chastellain's chronicle were recited at the Burgundian court before their publication. His reputation as the "pearl and star of the historiographers," which followed him well into the sixteenth century, may have been a recognition of the delight that the recitation of his text gave to successive generations of listeners. Did not La Marche envy him for the subtlety of his speech ("subtil parler")?[41] Whether or not all or part of Chastellain's chronicle was read aloud at the Burgundian court, Chastellain wrote it as if he intended it to be. Some of his most striking scenes are more dramatic (the death of Henry V of England, for example) because they are cast in dialogue form.[42] Much of his phrasing seems primarily intended for oral delivery ("Now I shall recite some of the lamentations uttered by the Duchess Michèle").[43] In his description of crowd scenes (royal processions, for example), he is more attentive to sound than to visual effects. As Henry V and Charles VI make their joint entry at Paris after the Treaty of Troyes in 1420, "one could hear them (the Parisian crowds) screaming at the top of their voices, laughing, crying, shouting hurrah, singing, saluting." Immediately behind the kings are their queens, who are greeted with "cries of Noël in a high voice, from every direction."[44] On a more austere occasion, the arrival of Louis XI's in Paris after his coronation at Rheims in 1461, the Parisian crowds are "expressly forbidden to shout," and find it difficult to "restrain their mouths from expressing what their eyes found worthy of such admiration."[45]

Though it would seem exaggerated to argue that Chastellain reduced the discipline of history to an elaborate rhetorical exercise, he did consider history as a parent if not a handmaiden of rhetoric and always brought his skills as a speaker to bear on the exposition of his subject. In keeping with a tradition that goes back to Cicero and Quintilian, he significantly placed history among the most "praiseworthy and glorious" items that are worth remembering. His broadest definition of *histoires* included "the noble sayings and the little-known treatises of the ancient philosophers, poets, orators; the heroic deeds and virtues of the great men of all ages and cultures since the beginning of the world."[46]

If Chastellain is understood correctly, historiography is a subordinate offshoot of literature. He did not consider the writing of history as an independent discipline with autonomous rules; rather he seems to have adopted a characteristic medieval attitude, first expressed by Isidore of Seville, that history is a by-product of grammar: "Haec disciplina ad grammaticam pertinet: quia quidquid dignum memoria est litteris mandatur."[47] Both Chastellain and La Marche considered it their secondary mission to record the past and their primary one to entertain a literary public. Chastellain even refuses to confer any utilitarian value upon his chronicle; nor does he place it alongside the necessary or even the useful baggage of the human mind. It is to be numbered among the "glorious and praiseworthy pursuits" and its fundamental end is "the soul's delight and sovereign contemplation."[48] La Marche, too, describes the purpose of his memoirs as "pleasure and delight"; his prologue reads like an exordium wherein, like a well-trained orator, he outlines the threefold division of his argument.[49]

Burgundian historiography, in keeping with the Ciceronian definition of history, is an "opus oratorium maxime."[50] Although it dealt with events that really took place ("res gestae"), its presentation was expected to contain the rhetorical and stylistic qualities of good oratory. The Burgundian historian's most pressing concern, in Chastellain's phrase, was "to set this subject matter down in an elegant, appropriate style." Its ultimate purpose was not essentially truth but literary delight ("avec affection que avoye à le complaire," as Chastellain says), and in this regard it had everything in common with rhetoric and poetry.[51]

In literature as in court the final beneficiary of flattery was the flatterer himself. "Kings change; kingdoms disappear; virtue and merit derived from labor are a man's only companion to the grave, his only guarantee of eternal glory. Such is the way I have always seen things; such is the cause and the aim of my work."[52] Chastellain made no secret of his desire to fashion a durable monument to himself; the people and events of his time, even the dukes, were little more to him, ultimately, than brick and mortar and bronze. Such was perhaps to be the court historiographer's posthumous revenge for years spent at court waiting officiously upon dukes and working his way through the ranks of intendance: he alone would have immortality and dwell in the unapproachable light of literary fame. The only "monumentum aere perennius" is the literary page; the chronicler alone stands between the court's present glory and its future dissolution. "I am writing and depicting for all time, present and future," wrote Chastellain, and elsewhere he described his purpose as that of "perpetuating him [Duke Philip], God willing."[53] Perpetuating the Burgundian court was the historiographers' privilege which even the dukes could never share with them. A pleasing literary style was their one assurance (or so they thought) of a permanent seat in the literary sky: satellites no more to the Burgundian sun, but stars of historiography burning forever with the light of their own merit.

They were doomed to fail, too self-conscious and far too obsequious for the tastes of the passionate few who keep the medieval tradition alive. One cannot be a Chastellain for one's contemporaries and expect to be a Saint-Simon for all time. The Burgundian play of mirrors yielded a brilliant but highly confusing labyrinth of images. Chastellain and Olivier both lacked the distance from their objective that assures sound judgment, and the distance from themselves that secures objective criticism. They continue now to attract occasional, isolated admirers who dust off their chronicles with a nostalgic hand; but unlike the reflection of Narcissus, these mirrors fire neither admiration nor consuming passion.

6 THOMAS BASIN: HISTORY
cum Ira et Studio

THOMAS BASIN was born in 1412 at Caudebec, a town in Normandy, of a rich merchant family.[1] An early display of intelligence and literary talent seemed to insure the success of whatever career he would choose. He received his Master of Arts degree at the University of Paris, at the exceptionally early age of seventeen, after which he obtained his licentiate in civil law at the University of Pavia and his licentiate in canon law at Louvain. At the age of twenty-three, Basin decided to enter the Church. His choice was based on a sincere conviction, and, in any case, it could only enhance his ambitions. In Rome, where he prepared for his ordination, Basin was welcomed by Pope Eugenius IV and "introduced into the society of the foremost scholars and men of letters, . . . the cream of the intellect in Christendom."[2] Having met and mingled with Poggio and his circle of humanists, Basin plunged into the study of Latin literature. When he returned to his native Normandy, his mind filled with classical and Italian letters and broadened by travel in Eastern Europe, Basin was appointed to a canonry in Rouen. In 1447, at the age of thirty-five, he was instituted bishop of Lisieux, by a bull of Pope Nicholas V.

The turning point in Basin's life came after Charles VII of France had decided to mount a campaign in order to recapture Normandy from the English, who had occupied the province since 1415. The young bishop, whose family had suffered greatly at the hands of the English since Agincourt, was only too happy to pay homage to the reconquering French sovereign. In 1454, the young dauphin (who was later to become King Louis XI) conspired to wrest Normandy from his father and sent written requests to the Norman bishops demanding their official approval. Basin did more than refuse the dauphin's requests; he dispatched the incriminating letters to Charles VII. The Spider King never forgave the bishop for this deed.

During the decade that followed Louis XI's accession to the French throne in 1461, Basin was persona non grata with the king. After being persecuted and tormented, Basin chose to go into exile. At Trier he wrote his history of the reign of Charles VII and began the history of the reign of Louis XI, both in Latin. When he died at Utrecht in 1491, Basin had not set foot on French soil in twenty years.

After the strained objectivity and the high-flown prose of the Burgundian chroniclers, Thomas Basin brings to medieval historiography a refreshing note of passion. His faults, which prompted the nineteenth-century editor and critic, Jules Quicherat, to call him an "unfair" chronicler, are the very qualities which might endear him to the amateur of medieval literature. "He lacks the gift of a free conscience, which allows one to judge the most tormenting situations as if one were not there. Thomas Basin was an upright, sincere, intelligent man; but he had too lively an imagination to see always in a lucid manner, too emotional a soul not to be often unfair."[3] But Basin had no reason to withdraw from his chronicle "as if he had not been there." He had dealt personally with Charles VII and Louis XI for many years. In 1454, he had personally foiled the young dauphin's plot to overthrow his father. For ten years after his accession to the throne, Louis XI had persecuted him, sent him on exhausting missions, forced him into exile. How could Basin write his memoirs of the two reigns as an impassive and benevolent spectator?

Historical writing is, to Basin's eye, a constant exercise in focusing, selection, and criticism.[4] "It was not my purpose," he argues, "to recount every single armed conflict, every siege, every assault and skirmish. To do so would surely have filled many large volumes. I included in my narrative what I considered most important and worthy of retention ['que graviora atque illustriora relatuque et memoria digniora reputavimus']. My account makes it sufficiently clear that the human condition is mobile, fragile, and subject to change. . . . What I have related of Charles [VII], king of France, and of his nephew, Henry [V] of England, bears me out."[5] Whereas a compilation of all the images that have come within the chronicler's field of vision in his lifetime could have filled many volumes, historical writing must be a selective montage composed only of those events that are by nature *graviora, illustriora, digniora*. Basin refuses to adopt an egalitarian style, which would make of the chronicler an impassive or amused secretary, recording in a linear monotone. He does not—and here he differs fundamentally from Froissart and the Burgundians—picture history as a horizontal surface and events as so many objects placed side by side. He usually does not dwell either on physical events or states of consciousness. Nor does he project on each chosen event a light of uniform intensity. Some details are set in high relief while others, once mentioned, are quickly overshadowed. Most visually colorful moments, which would have filled dozens of pages in the Burgundian chronicles, are dismissed quickly and almost with impatience. While Olivier de la Marche spends more than a hundred pages describing the wedding feast of Duke Charles of Burgundy and Princess Margaret of York, Basin deals with it in a few lines: "To relate all the details of such a splendid feast," he explains, "is not in keeping with my purpose. [I shall leave] that task to historians with a talent for such things."[6] The battle of Montlhéry is dismissed in a paragraph; but it takes several chapters to justify the moral and political intentions of the coalition that led to it.[7] The treaty of Péronne is handled not as a dramatic scene, but as a highly significant document.[8]

A rigorous preliminary selection, a sense of focus proportionate to the importance of the event, an intellectual montage: history is, in every sense of the word, a "critical" discipline. The historian is both judge and participant; he can raise his voice, interpret, exhort, condemn. Rarely does Basin recount the simplest historical fact without injecting a clear or disquieting note of judgment. Facts are rarely presented visually and uncritically, as with Froissart. By the time the historical detail reaches the reader, it has been screened by the historian's critical judgment. An apparently harmless declaration, such as: "After the death of Charles VII, king of France, Louis, his eldest son, succeeded him on the throne," rarely passes without comment or interpretation: "An inheritor, no doubt, of his lands and his patrimony, yet, alas! how lacking he was in prudence, loyalty, justice, and the other paternal virtues!"[9]

Basin knows that he cannot take up the historian's pen without indulging in criticism. Most chronicles before him have yielded either tedious if useful factual records or annoying "chroniques élogieuses." An unaccustomed public might easily mistake intelligent history for diatribe. "At the time I began to write [the *History of Louis XI*]," he confesses, "I felt doubtful and uncertain. . . . I was afraid, in fact, that by revealing his subtle, malicious, perfidious, sottish, pernicious, and cruel deeds, some of our readers, little inclined to take us at our word, might take me for a slanderer rather than a historian. . . . [Yet] I far prefer to employ my leisure time instructing and cautioning posterity with a truthful narrative than to lend an ear to lies and fables, as the flatterers and the panegyrists have done."[10]

How to exercise one's critical sense while resisting the oversimplifications of the panegyrists at one end of the historiographical spectrum and of the slanderers on the other, how to steer a clear course between oversimplification of reality and its deliberate complication, both of which are characteristic of legend: such is Basin's dilemma, and such is his talent. While his rapier-like mind is ever cutting through the fat of historical detail, he remains aware of the complexity of most historical issues. He condemns the despotic tendencies of Charles VII when he sees fit to do so, and considers the king's creation of a permanent army of *franci sagittarii,* or tax-exempt archers, as an unhappy precedent which can only diminish the freedom of the citizens; yet his overriding attitude toward the eponymous hero of his chronicle (whom he sometimes refers to as "illustris Francorum rex") is one of admiration.[11]

His astonishingly accurate account of the life and death of Joan of Arc, written only forty years after her death, manages to avoid both the pious oversimplifications of hagiography and the idle curiosity of the roving journalist.[12] Basin realizes that Joan's story is a complicated one and that forty years of notoriety have already covered the facts of her case with a crust of suppositions and old wives' tales. While limiting himself to those facts of which he is sure, Basin follows Joan through her extraordinarily active career, from the peaceful days at Domremy, through the tempestuous trial, to the stake at Rouen. In discussing the sensitive matter of her virginity, he makes no concessions to prudery or morbid curiosity. "She affirmed that she had consecrated her virginity to God; and although she had spent a long time in the company of soldiers and dissolute men, she was never accused of having broken her vow. Moreover, when she was captured by the English, she was inspected by midwives to determine whether she was intact. They reported that she had remained absolutely chaste. She justified her wearing men's clothes by saying that God had ordered her to wear them and to don armor. She did not wish to excite the lustful desires of the men with whom she would have to live night and day during her campaigns. . . . But, of course, whatever the virtues she exemplified, how could she possibly justify herself to her captors, when their most ardent wish was to do away with her?"[13]

Basin is neither too selective nor too generous in his choice of historical detail. Concrete events are never sacrificed to some ogre-like general thesis, nor does the reader lose sight of a topic under discussion in a maze of unconnected trivia. Too much simplification of one's field of vision impoverishes the mind and rigidifies the chronicle. Too great a receptivity leads to verbal prolixity and ideological confusion. Basin owes his freedom as historian to the fact that he seems equally distant from preconceived theses and from ideological indifference. His mind is neither Protean nor Procrustean.

His dramatis personae, like their author, are flexible, dynamic figures with a strong imprint of freedom and personality. Like the sculptured faces of late Gothic architecture, they have retained little of the stylized attitudes of Villehardouin's, Joinville's, even Froissart's characters. Facial and verbal expressions are less stilted than they were in previous chronicles; and although characters, situations, and speeches may be fraught with tension, they are rarely awkward. To consider a characteristically suspenseful and dramatic moment in the *History of Charles VII:* the Norman bishops have just foiled the young dauphin's plot to overthrow his father, Charles VII; the young Louis, fearing his life is in danger, flees into Burgundian territory. Charles VII sends several ambassadors, on repeated occasions, to the Burgundian duke, asking him to cease providing asylum for his son. Upon the duke's answer depends the continuation of an already strained political friendship with the king, his cousin. Yet Philip also realizes that the dauphin's right to sanctuary is inviolable, even if there is no immediate political advantage to be gained in protecting him. The confrontation between the duke and the king's ambassadors is consequently filled with background detail, historical complexity, and dramatic tension. The threads of such a complicated tapestry are difficult to unravel, yet the duke manages with an admirable dexterity. His reply to his cousin, being sent by way of a messenger, is appropriately narrated in the indirect discourse:

> But as for chasing his son [Louis XI] from his domain, to which the dauphin had fled for fear of his father, without his requesting it in any way, or even wishing it, Philip of Burgundy maintained that he could not in honesty accede to the king's wish. . . . He would, he said, be incurring the eternal dishonor of the loyal subjects of his duchy and of all those capable of appraising the situation correctly; moreover, he would be making of the dauphin an enemy for all time since, in the natural order of things, he could expect him to become king some day. What a crime it would be against the law of nations if Philip allowed himself to betray the young man who, with confidence in his humanity and goodness, had taken refuge in his duchy. . . . Was he to hand him over to a father from whom he had taken refuge under the seal of human confidence? If the dauphin thought him capable of such a deed . . . he would perhaps escape to some territory of his father's enemies. The king should remember that the duke's favor to the dauphin was being done not so much for the son

as for the father and for the royal house of France, from which Philip himself was descended.[14]

The speech is repetitious, flowery, perhaps too self-conscious in its search for symmetry, like flamboyant Gothic. But despite the euphemisms, there is a dramatic tension here, and it centers about Philip of Burgundy, whose power and influence stand between an arrogant dauphin and an irate king. Torn between the need to keep an unbreakable promise of hospitality and the necessity to shore up a fragile political friendship, his mind works freely and swiftly, in an attempt to parry both the arguments presented and the eventual counterobjections. Appealing to immediate, concrete, and human ideas and feelings, foregoing no rhetorical effect that might serve his purpose, Philip performs with an admirable mental dexterity. His argument is a continuous, uninterrupted fabric; there are no breaks, no silences in his argument to be filled in by the reader. A free agent serving as arbiter between other free agents, Philip is the meeting point of personalities, which, like the human condition itself, are in Basin's own words, *lubrica, fragilis, versatilis*. He is at the center of a dynamic confrontation of wills. Caught between Charles's request and the dauphin's refusal, the duke alleges the impartiality of his own desire while in fact indulging in a highly active exercise of will.

French historiography has made considerable strides in expressing the complexity of human situations. One recalls the unanswered questions remaining after Villehardouin's rigid account of the confrontation between the French barons and their army at Zara; or the charming but stilted dialogue between Louis IX and Joinville over the matter of leprosy and mortal sin, and Joinville's awkward silences. Basin has retained their sense of discretion, selectivity, and judgment while surpassing them in animation and syntactical fluidity. And while he has few of Froissart's or Chastellain's talent for description and motion, he has a far better sense of the historically relevant detail.

Basin is most sensitive to historical development. While time affects Froissart's or Chastellain's characters only as an exterior measurement of things, few of Basin's people remain unaware of its power to mold, develop, or destroy. Friendships, like enmities, are sustained by time and memory. Time develops personal awareness, consecrates ancient alliances, and can even favor reconciliations.[15] Great events always belong to a historical context. A significant battle like Agincourt, for example, is more than a timeless "haut fait d'armes," with nothing at stake but personal honor and abundant spoils. It is a historic encounter of free men, and their leaders know that the political future of two great nations is at stake. More than a piece of chivalric bravado, King Henry V's exhortation to his troops is a realistic evaluation of the present historical picture, solidly shored up by experience and foresight:

> The time has come, my good and valiant comrades in arms, when you will have to fight not for the glory and honor of your name, but for life itself. We, who know the presumptuous state of mind of the French, are certain that if, out of cowardice or fear, you allow them to defeat us, they will spare none of you. They will kill you, noble or plebeian, as they would cattle. For myself and the princes of my blood, we are not afraid this will happen to us; for if they defeat us, they will be careful to keep us alive rather than destroy us, in the hope of obtaining great sums of gold. As for yourselves, if you wish to avoid such a danger, dismiss all fear from your hearts. Do not entertain the hope that the enemy will keep you so as to allow you to ransom your lives with money: they have always hated our race with an inveterate and bitter hatred. Therefore, if it is better to live than die, be courageous, remembering your ancient nobility and English glory in other wars. Fight like men, valiantly and courageously, for the safeguard of your souls.[16]

One is immediately tempted to compare a speech like this one to any of Chastellain's prepared discourses. Locked in static if colorful poses (like human figures in fifteenth-century Flemish tapestries), Chastellain's speakers have little or no sense of the historical relevance of their words; they do little else than reflect the rhetorical prowess of their creator. Basin's King Henry, on the other hand, though his text may be Sallustian in flavor, is a dynamic, fluid actor with an extraordinary intuition as to the significance of the moment.[17]

Whether he is describing the valor of the English in northern France during the decade following Agincourt or the astounding French military revival after 1435, Basin depicts live, mobile characters, never passively led around, making of impersonal fate a personal destiny. His highest praise seems reserved for active, resilient men like Charles VII who, when he hears the seemingly crushing news of the fall of Bordeaux to the English (in October 1452), "thought [*cogitavit*] immediately of the remedy that was needed. And since winter was setting in . . . the king dispatched [*misit*] troops into each city and castle [under his control]. . . . But he put off [*constituit*] until the following summer any plan to carry the war into territory occupied by the English."[18] Basin's use of active preterites like *cogitavit, misit, constituit* suggests the firmness and the immediacy of the king's decisions. There is an admirable crispness to passages like these, as actions are described in brisk, trenchant terms.

A complex art, the writing of history must be guided by intelligence, and the final document must be intelligible. Basin's mind functions conceptually rather than esthetically; the basic purpose of his text is to impress knowledge upon the reader's mind. In favoring this conception of hisory, Basin betrays his classically inspired bent for rationality. History is texture, and the real historian's job is to unravel and reweave the strands so as to make the fabric intelligible. The center of the fabric can be attained only if the historian has begun at the outer edges— which may not be a good rule of weaving but does make for solid history. In justifying the amount of space he has allotted to the reign of Charles VI (1380–1422) at the start of his *History of Charles VII,* Basin argues that "to understand the evils [of the reign of Charles VII], one must necessarily reconstruct our civic discords at their root and origin. . . . I have not thought it unreasonable to place the foundation of my narrative so far back. Indeed, the murder of the duke of Orléans, the fountainhead of all the subsequent ills in the kingdom, occurred during that reign."[19]

Whether history be metaphorically featured as a fabric to be reconstructed, an edifice to be sustained (*fundamentum*), or an organism whose roots plunge far back in time, Basin's imagery suggests a common truth: in order to provide intelligibility, the historian's intellect must begin by disassembling the constituent part of an event. Somewhere amid the fragments there is a key moment, a fundamental starting point projecting on subsequent events the light of intelligibility.

Intelligibility, therefore, is not a product made up by some *historicus faber,* molding an absurd or amorphous mass, but an adequation between historical mind and historical matter; it is inscribed in the historical fabric like some design in filigree on a tapestry; but the historian, in unraveling the fabric, must find it. Basin's history is like a complex musical score; if left uninterpreted, or if interpreted incorrectly, it might seem like an absurd cacophony or a series of meaningless symbols. The historian as performing artist must replace the composer and retrace his omniscience. Simply to record, for example, that "King Louis XI sent ambassadors to the duke of Burgundy" is insufficient; the historian must add (for this, too, is historically real) that the king's hidden purpose was "to dispel any suspicion of ruse or treachery on his part."[20] Both physical and psychological events are related with the same degree of certitude. It is for somewhat the same reasons that Basin makes such frequent use of indirect discourse: it allows him to narrate with two voices, the first of which relates while the other interprets motives and significances, injects comments, and detects silences.[21]

As a result (and whatever be its weaknesses), Bishop Basin's chronicle is one of the most intelligible in medieval French historiography. He remains ever above the events of his time, the complexity of which sometimes defeats more attractive chroniclers. How clear, for example, is his account of the battle of Montlhéry, which even Commynes, a brilliant but dizzied participant, never manages to decipher through the dust, the smoke, and the heat![22] How concise his summary of the treaty of Péronne! Commynes's account is perhaps more picturesque (especially when he describes Duke Charles's fits of anger), but he is standing too close to the event to be able to see it in the right perspective. Basin, considering the same event from a distance, is less visually colorful than Commynes, but far clearer in summarizing the provisions of the treaty and their political significance.[23]

The historian's mind must feel free to speculate over historical matter, to rearrange the past in a variety of real and possible combinations. Once past, historical facts are lifeless butterflies pinned to a collector's board; the historian must bring them back to life, examine the hidden factors, even speculate as to what might have happened had variables such as free will been used differently. Basin pushes the intelligibility of history to the point of making speculative assertions on cases which are grammatically conditional and contrary to fact. Given other hypotheses (expressed in "conditionally pluperfect" form), Basin is certain of what the outcome of an event would have been. He is quite as assertive about his characters' hidden motives of action.[24]

He does not offer opinions, however, on problems that leave him reasonably unsure, and he shows an habitual aversion to making pronouncements as to suppositions that smack of bigotry. Is the English victory at Agincourt to be interpreted as a sign of God's revenge upon the French for pillaging the monastry at Soissons? Was the battle not fought on the feast day of Saints Crispin and Crispinian? And was the monastery not placed under the protecting guidance of these same blessed martyrs? "Let people think what they will," Basin replies. "For myself, I shall be satisfied to give a true account of what happened and leave to those who entertain such presumptions the task of discussing the arcane workings of divinity."[25] Basin dismisses a contemptible hypothesis with a whiplash stroke of his pen: "De quo senciet quisque prout voluerit." The anonymous and worthless nature of the pious suppositions is implied, so far as the author is concerned, by his use of an impersonal construction in the passive voice: "Unde creditum est."[26]

A resolute defender of intelligibility, Bishop Basin is perhaps (along with Commynes) the French medieval chronicler whose assertions make the most universal claims. The history of his time is but a series of concrete instances illustrating universal historical truths, as his major characters illustrate universal human types. The maintenance of a permanent army of paid soldiers by Charles VII is, to be sure, an instance of abuse of power in a certain kingdom, France, at a particular point in time, the mid-fifteenth century, but the event radiates a universal message which is valid for the past as for the future, for France as for the rest of Europe: "As free men, let us freely obey any prince who governs justly and legitimately for the good of all, and let us give him our allegiance. But if one governs neither justly nor legitimately nor for the general welfare, but in order to sacrifice the republic to his private, iniquitous, and unjust passions, and to reduce his subjects to abject slavery, it is far better not to obey him. If the power to resist him were given us, we should be doing a far worthier thing than if, with a dumb patience, we were to put up with his wild and unjust lusts and passions, as if we were approving them."[27] A single event can thus provide a springboard for a condensed philosophy of political revolution; and Basin's personal preoccupation with the maintenance of ecclesiastical privilege is both sublimated and universalized into a categorical imperative.[28]

His wide use of classical historical models is another factor contributing to the universality of his message. From the very first lines of the *History of Charles VII,* the reader is plunged into a literary tradition whose most ancient referents are Sallust, Suetonius, and Cicero. A reader who is at all familiar with the Roman historians is tempted to compare some of Basin's scenes with their classical models, like pictures in an imaginary museum. A dramatic confrontation between Duke Philip the Good, the young dauphin, and his father reads almost like a scene in a Senecan tragedy. (Basin quotes Seneca's tragedies more than a dozen times in his complete works.) King Henry's speech to his troops on the eve of the battle of Agincourt is highly reminiscent of Catiline's speech before his last battle against Antony, in Sallust's *De Coniuratione Catilinae*.

Basin also shores up his deepest philosophical convictions with classical references so as to give them the widest possible validity. Were he to support his argumentation with scriptural or medieval text alone, he would be indulging in a provincialism of the mind which as a cosmopolitan humanist he wishes studiously to avoid. When he argues in favor of man's instinctive desire for political freedom, for example, Basin realizes that he is advocating a political ideal that Sallust and Cicero would have defended as warmly as Saint Paul. The political scene in France during the reign of Charles VII offers some parallels with that of imperial Rome, but it would be pointless, he argues, to justify a present abuse on the grounds that it was current practice in the past. Historical parallels are helpful only to those who realize that circumstances are never quite the same.

> Let no one allege, in order to convince me that this army of ours is necessary in time of peace as in time of war, that the Romans at the peak of their power always had legions at their command . . . and that the kings of the ancient Assyrian, Mede, Persian, and Egyptian empires had armies ever prepared for war. I would answer "true," but they did not have a reserve army of nobles within their provincial territories; or if they did, it was so small as to be insufficient to protect the empire. Moreover, these empires were founded on violence and conquered with the force of arms. They had deprived whole populations of their natural freedom and enslaved them. In order to last they had to maintain these captive populations with the same means they had used in subduing them. But, as Cicero says so eloquently, "No power can last if it is founded on fear." It is clear that these empires were set up neither in accordance with nature nor with the consent of the governed, since, whenever the occasion arose, these subjects shook off the yoke of tyranny and won back their ancient freedom, so that almost all of these empires finished by passing away. . . . What man freely born, in fact, could bear without protest to be reduced to such a degree of servitude that the privilege of possessing anything that is not in keeping with the prince's wishes would be taken from him? . . . Love of freedom is natural to every man. Hardly are we in the world than we already aspire to possess it. As Cicero says: "No spirit well constituted by nature will ever consent to obey anyone who does not provide a model, or teach, or govern for a right cause."[29]

In this, his most eloquent statement in defense of man's right to autonomy, Basin quotes Cicero three times. The whole argument reads like a long passage from the *De Officiis,* capped by an anticlimactic appeal to Saint Paul for religious confirmation. Basin seems clearly to feel on more solid ground with Cicero than with the Apostle; and his appeal to the first letter to the Corinthians is both ambiguous and unconvincing.[30]

History, therefore, can and must be philosophical. Like his Roman models the spectator-chronicler must learn how to step away from his immediate perception of single events; the distance thus gained enables him to transform images into ideas and individual instances into universal structures. A Christian Stoic in his moral views (he quotes Cicero more often than he does Saint Paul), Basin is aware of a "distance" of another kind that separates what the Stoics called *bona exteriora* from the *interiora,* and transient historical glory from metaphysical and religious certitude.

Like writing good history, living the good life is largely a matter of learning to keep a proper distance; from his retreat at Trier, an exiled bishop who will never again see his native Normandy realizes that courageous writers have often had some distances forced upon them. An apparent failure in time, he clings jealously to the precious, timeless notion of substance. He is ever ready to argue that if men are to be judged not according to what they are but to what they have, if men's actions are to be evaluated not according to their intent but to their result, then history is indeed a sorry tale of frustrated heroism and defeated sanctity. No, the coalition of French nobles who attempted to overthrow the "tyrant," Louis XI, was right, though it failed; and the apostles were right, though many were crucified.[31]

But Basin's pen alone could not vindicate him entirely. He was too deeply hurt by his repudiation and exile ever to achieve a final though bitter serenity. He rarely resisted the temptation to mistake his pen for a rapier, nor could he forego the immediate satisfactions of an occasionally savage irony. His *History of Louis XI* is admittedly an attempt to unmask the Spider King, to show him for what he really was; but Basin was far too abrasive, too fundamentally honest, to master the art of saying the opposite of what he meant. His irony, too irate and too bitter, turns out to be more soul-destroying than effective. In the very passages in which he tries his hand at cynicism, he confesses that his soul is an open wound, and he is never serene enough to feign indifference toward the bishopric and the privileges of which he has been dispossessed.

To the very end of his chronicles, Basin refused to believe in the pusillanimity of God; but he did argue for certain forms of divine retribution in history. Providence seemed to him inseparable from a theory of historical justice. The highest mark of the intrusion of the *divinum opus* in time is that love should spring where formerly there was hatred between enemies. Yet Basin injects into his theology a disquieting mark of transcendence: for if Providence embraces all historical events, it seems disturbingly *laissez-faire* with the frequently destructive mechanisms of necessity and chance. If all of history is "directed by a divinity which sees and regulates all things from on high," the lower part of the mechanism seems to work by itself, an autonomous field of analysis and speculation.[32] Basin is remarkably sober, even reticent, in rendering judgments that presuppose the presence of the supernatural in the historical order.

His implicit sense of the hierarchy of being seems, finally, to lead him into a number of contradictions. An acute critical sense works harmoniously with a seemingly profound faith; a Christian bishop refuses to accept most of the miracles witnessed by the *vulgus* of his time; an exiled Stoic recommends detachment from the things of the world yet remonstrates violently against a king who overtaxed him and forced him to detach himself; a Christian historian views all of history as a "divinum opus," yet his view of the divinity is so telescopic that man seems left in a cosmic semi-loneliness, to suffer exile, shame, and death at the hands of cruel men.

These contradictions may simply be the mark of a civilized mind. If Basin's chronicle is judged as historical document alone, it is a curious but dated text. If evaluated as a private vision of reality in the late fifteenth century, the work cannot be dismissed so cavalierly, especially because of its ability to describe the "humanarum rerum condicio" in its "ondoyante et diverse," confused, even contradictory reality. Basin's examination of a welter of historical events yields neither crystalline design nor total darkness; his characters seem the protagonists of a developing drama, the meaning and outcome of which are yet unclear to the narrator. History is a tale told neither by an idiot nor by a logician, and the most intelligible tales are those told by free, sensitive, dynamic men who have the courage to love their destiny.

This is not to say that Basin considers action as the royal way to truth. Historical truth is not a subjective exercise in creation. Historiography is, in its authentic sense, a record of one's creative fidelity to fact, a "veridica narracio"; it is the historian's privilege to write "cum ira et studio" if he so wishes, but he must manage to avoid the "vana et mendosa scripta" told by lying, flattering chroniclers who lack the courage to be truly irate and the talent to be truly "studious."[33] Basin's anger is, in sum, the best guarantee of his freedom and independence of thought. In his remarkable preface to the *History of Charles VII,* where the words *veritas, veridica narracio,* and *verum* are conspicuous in their opposition to *mendacium* and *mendosa scripta,* he argues unequivocally, if implicitly, that an angry historian need not be indifferent to truth. His chronicle of the reigns of Charles VII and Louis XI represented a sincere effort to bear out this claim. Despite his contradictions, he remains, along with Commynes, one of the most intelligent minds in fifteenth-century France.

7 COMMYNES: HISTORY AS LOST INNOCENCE

PHILIPPE DE COMMYNES (1447–1511) has been variously referred to as the successor to Thucydides, the precursor of Machiavelli, and the first "truly modern" French historian.[1] Named squire to Charles the Bold in 1464, he fought at the battle of Montlhéry, where he discovered that "the art of fleeing in time is as important as the art of fighting." After the death of Duke Philip the Good of Burgundy (1467), Commynes became the most trusted counsellor to Charles the Bold, the fourth and last of the great Burgundian dukes. At Péronne, in 1468, while attempting to reconcile Duke Charles with Louis XI, he is thought to have accepted a substantial "gift" from the Spider King. It was not until August 1472, however, that he defected from the Burgundian court to serve the king of France.

Louis XI saw to it that Commynes would never regret his decision. In addition to a pension of six thousand pounds, he was given the title of king's counsellor and chamberlain. For five years, from 1472 until 1477, he was the king's most important and trusted minister. He contributed to the success of the encounter between Louis XI and Edward IV of England at Picquigny in 1475; the treaty signed there spared England and France yet another round of perhaps century-long warfare. In 1478 Commynes was assigned an important mission to the court of Lorenzo de Medici in Florence, and there he became acquainted with the devious art of Italian diplomacy and politics. Although he had fallen somewhat from favor after 1478, he was one of the few persons admitted to witness the physical and moral decline of Louis XI, who died on August 30, 1483.

During the regency that followed (1483–91), Commynes fell pro-

gressively into disfavor. Forced to restore to the La Trémoïlle family
the property of Talmont, which Louis XI had given him as a reward
for his desertion in 1472, Commynes conspired against the regents
(Anne de Bretagne and René de Lorraine) along with the dukes of
Bourbon and Orléans. He was arrested in 1487, imprisoned for more
than twenty months, then sentenced to a forced retirement in his estate
at Dreux in March 1489. It was during this period of imprisonment and
exile that he wrote most of the first six books of his *Mémoires,* dealing
with the reign of Louis XI (1461–83).

With the accession of Charles VIII to the throne in 1491, Commynes
returned to court, but he never regained the prestige he had enjoyed
two decades earlier. Although he was opposed to the young king's designs on the kingdom of Naples—an ambition dating back to Duke
Charles of Anjou's conquest of the Kingdom of the Two Sicilies in 1265
—Commynes accompanied the king's expeditionary force into Italy in
1494. He was sent to Venice in order to dissuade the doge from engaging in war against the French invaders; he managed to secure Venetian neutrality, but he could not prevent Venice from joining a defensive, anti-French coalition called the Holy League. Commynes was
present at the battle of Fornovo in July 1495 and witnessed the treaty of
Vercelli in the same year.

Charles VIII died prematurely in 1498 and was succeeded by Louis
XII, the former duke of Orléans. Commynes hoped that his former
friend and fellow conspirator during the regency days, "a man for whom
I had suffered so many troubles and losses," would be mindful of his
past friendship and favors. "Toutesfoiz, pour l'heure, ne luy en souvint
point fort." Until his death on October 18, 1511, Commynes spent
most of his declining years away from court, quibbling with neighbors
and vassals over legal matters of estate and ownership.[2]

Commynes was a realist in both a moral and an epistemological
sense. Perhaps his most characteristic feature, in contradistinction to
Froissart, is that he systematically transforms sense perception into universal cognition. Unlike his nominalist predecessor, Commynes views
history not as a great chain of monadic incidents but as a residue of
knowledge, principally moral, that can be distilled from those incidents.
His project, announced in the opening lines of his Prologue, is to commit to writing "what I have known," and to make it "as close to the
truth as I can."[3] His affinity for substance is as pronounced as was
Froissart's for incidentals. His occasional anecdotes or digressions are
perceptively distinguished from the substantive message, "la matière
principale."[4] An Aristotelian who perhaps never read Aristotle, his uni-

versals are composites formed by extracting the characteristics common to each of the singulars. His idea of a "prince," for example, is the product of a long association with princes, and he creates this fragile concept with the assiduousness of a bee gathering honey from flowers: "Any man who could have taken a part of the characteristics of the king our Master [Louis XI] and a part of the duke's [Charles of Burgundy] could have made a perfect prince."[5] Like Basin, Commynes looks upon history as a pursuit of intelligibility; his world of time, motion, and sense, once stripped of its outer shell, reveals a structured, irreducible core of timeless truth. He is, in the Aristotelian sense of the word, an "intellectus agens," an active intellect.

An immediate consequence of the highly cognitive structure of Commynes's mind is his insisting that the object of historical writing (considered whether in the making or in the end product) is truth. As a historian at work, comparing, weighing, and judging, Commynes has "decided not to speak of anything which is not true and which I have not seen or heard from such great people that they are worthy of being believed."[6] "I believe that I have seen and known the greater part of Europe."[7] It follows that the end product of the historian's inquiry, the book, is also intended to produce truth in the mind of the reader. A young prince of future days into whose hands Commynes's *Memoirs* might fall, "having seen this . . . may gain a better understanding of these things and guard himself against deceit."[8]

Rarely does one find in any of the medieval French chroniclers a deeper respect for the written document. Experience, asserts this man of action who had little time to read, does not suffice to attain wisdom. A single life is far too short to accumulate the experiences contained in historical documents. One of the best ways of educating a young prince in the ways of moral and political wisdom is to read the documents of the past and to teach him to conduct himself according to the examples of our forebears contained in these histories. One can derive more experience from a single book in three months' time than twenty men, living successively, could ever see and experience ("veoir à l'oeil et entendre par experience").[9]

Such an admission from a warrior and diplomat might seem astounding, but it does prove the depth of his respect for the written word (it may have been during his active life as diplomat that Commynes noticed the inadequacy of his formal education) and it does show how deep was his personal taste for intellectual cognition. Commynes was by nature an intellectual, whether he had chosen to be or not. He could never have been a purely esthetic man; his vision is never arrested by the sense object itself; rarely does he employ the verb *veoir* without its being complemented by *sçavoir*. In brief, Commynes (somewhat like Villehardouin, although with a different method) can never see an object without at the same time seeing through it.

His images, therefore, are rarely the visual kind. His only occasional metaphors are a clashing encounter of concrete and moral imagery. The king's archers at the battle of Montlhéry were "the flower and the hope" of the royal army; in allowing themselves to be attacked while off guard and unarmed by the Burgundians at Montlhéry, "they themselves destroyed the flower of their hope."[10] At Liège, before the attacking armies of Burgundy and France the Liégeois fly from their own city by night, "for night knows no shame."[11]

Commynes's descriptions, like his metaphors, are punctuated by interpretive cognitive elements. His famous portraits, whether they be rapid sketches of the dukes of Burgundy and Brittany or a long, "official" portrait of Louis XI, are almost exclusively composed of moral elements.[12] Unlike Froissart, Commynes was too imbued with an ethical sense (whatever the morality of his own historical role may have been) to play the innocent, esthetic spectator in the face of any spectacle. Even his description of the sacked city of Liège—he must have officially approved the destruction of this recalcitrant city by Charles of Burgundy and, in any case, any objection on his part would have gone unheeded—cannot be presented to the reader without some measure of interpretation, moral awareness, or "mauvaise conscience":

> It was dreadful to hear the noise of the houses falling and crumbling in the town that night, for we heard it as clearly, being four leagues away, as if we had been there on the spot. I do not know whether it was because the wind was blowing in our direction or because we were camping on the banks of the river.
> The next day, after the duke was gone, those who had remained in the town continued with their destruction, according to their orders; but all the churches were saved, with a few exceptions, as well as more than three hundred houses belonging to the ecclesiastics. This is the reason why the city was repopulated so soon, for many people came to take refuge with the priests.
> . . . He [Charles] had all the houses burned, and all the iron-mills of the region (which were their chief means of livelihood) broken. . . .
> I saw incredible things resulting from the cold. One gentleman lost the use of his foot and never regained it; two fingers fell off from the hand of a page. I saw a woman who had died of cold, together with her newborn child.[13]

Even if Commynes did not punctuate his description with parenthetical signs of moral awareness, his very choice of visual details would betray his conviction that the historical spectacle does not justify itself on purely esthetic grounds and that the historian places moral and cognitive values above purely visual ones.

So consistently does Commynes point to the intelligible patterns of history, so pointedly does he underline the supreme value of intelligence (*sens, sçavoir, saigesse*) as a means of rising above singular events, that the reader might initially be tempted to conclude that his is a static world where the intelligible alone is real. This is not the case. The Commynian universe is far from rational. Human reason is loosely connected to a violent organism, like a precious bubble floating on stormy waters. Man's emotional states—fear, terror, illness—can influence or determine the tenor of his ideas, and in the depths of the psyche there crouches a persistent aggressiveness, unchecked by any law, whether human or divine: "One must conclude that neither our natural reason, nor our sense, nor fear of God, nor love of neighbor will restrain us at all from doing violence to one another, or from keeping for ourselves what belongs to another, or from taking the possessions of others by all possible means."[14]

Here lies the conflicting nature of Commynian man: he strains toward a timeless rationality while acknowledging his biological roots and their capacity for creating, coloring, and distorting ideas. He realizes that abstract cognition is inseparable though distinct from a consciousness of time. His capacity for conceptual thinking seems closely related to his ability to sense duration. The mental act enabling him to synthesize his experience and transcend his perception of singulars is identical with the act enabling him to assume consciousness of his past. To be conscious, in a Commynian sense, means to be conscious of time and to sense time as an uninterrupted inner flow.

Commynes has two conceptions of time. There are moments in his chronicle (as in any) when time is a unit of measure: such and such an event lasts three days or two weeks or "the space of more than two pater nosters."[15] But linear time is but an analogous, imperfect reflection of real time: "I am not observing the order of writing used in histories, and I am not mentioning the years of the exact times during which these events took place. . . . Since you have lived at the time when these events came to pass you have no need of being told with precision at what hour or season these things took place."[16]

Commynian time, in this second sense, is consciousness of self-duration and self-identity through the continuity of past experience: "from the time when I came into his service to the hour of his death, at which I was present, I have been at his side more continuously than anyone else."[17] Commynian man's states of consciousness—his perceptions, passions, cognitions, most of his interior experiences—are suffused with time, in this sense. Unlike Froissart, Commynes rarely projects his descriptions of states of consciousness into a metaphorical space.[18] Cognition is not the act of seizing a singular truth at a certain point along the line of time, but the ripening and growth of experience, like an inner garden. One could divide Commynes's dramatis personae between those who learn from their experience in time and those who fail to learn. Even a "hardly valiant" man like the emperor of Germany "had good judgment . . . and because of his long life, he was able to accumulate much experience."[19] The connétable de Saint Pol, on the other hand, or King Charles VIII or King Alfonso of Naples are men to whom time brought no accumulation of wisdom; as for Duke Charles of Burgundy, he suffered from a tragic disharmony between his boundless ambition and the time needed to bring it to fruition: "For he had so many great plans in mind that he could never have lived long enough to put all of them into execution; furthermore, they were practically impossible to realize, for half of Europe would not have been sufficient to satisfy him."[20]

Time, then, is not a juxtaposition but a fusion of interior states. To act in time, in a Commynian sense, is to be aware of the role played by time in bringing human intentions to maturity or to nothing. Indeed, most of Commynes's characters, like sprinters at the starting line, are intently poised in strained expectation of the future. Commynes's narrative is filled with purpose clauses, a syntactical indication that his characters act in and through time. Time is both the medium through which action is executed and the obstacle to its accomplishment. If action impels the Commynian character toward the future, passions like fear and hatred force him into an awareness of past states of consciousness that are being prolonged by the present moment. Fear is the most malignant of moral tumors, and its growth is one of the more telling signs of interior continuity.

Hatred, a corroding passion deeply rooted in the past, so fills the soul to overflowing that it appears to encompass it. It is a passion deeply marked by continuity;[21] it can never be eradicated from the heart until satisfied;[22] like a slow flame, it can be stirred and renewed ("lequel de tout temps *hayoit* . . . et la hayne estoit *renouvellée*").[23]

Commynes's ability to express simultaneous states of consciousness in time is one of the striking features of his art. Unlike Froissart, who quantifies actions, passions, and sensations like so many points along a line, Commynes succeeds in translating the non-spatial, diffuse quality of plural states of consciousness. The Commynian character's consciousness can be filled at the same time with fear, anger, and hatred; so un-localized is the passion that it seems to overflow the psyche itself and encompass it: "I have never known of any man who came to good after having tried to frighten his master or any great prince with whom he had dealings and to keep him in subjection. . . . And although every-one tries to free himself from subjection and fear, and hates those who keep him in that state, no one can compare with princes in this respect, for I have never known any who did not have a mortal hatred for those who attempted to maintain them in such a condition."[24]

Commynian man, then, is totally immersed in history; time, for him, is some sort of inner worm, gnawing away at his future while digesting his past and keeping it alive. The worm leaves its ravages along the way, and it can be as cruel and irrefutable as death itself: "I do not know toward whom Our Lord showed the greatest anger: toward him, who died suddenly on the battlefield, without lingering for long, or to-ward his subjects, who have never since enjoyed prosperity or peace."[25]

Curiously enough, Commynes's characters remain unresigned to the corrosive effects of human time. Why is this so? It is not their religious faith, surely, that softens the horror of death, for none of the main characters seems especially sensitive to the consolatory character of the afterlife.[26] Commynes's characters—the chronicler included—live with the willful conviction that time is not a passive, downhill slide. There comes a privileged moment, an eruption in the life of the Com-mynian character when he arbitrarily decides to smash the Procrustean machinery of a repetitive past. A rapid and paradoxical moment of rup-ture, when one assumes full consciousness of the past at the very mo-ment one breaks its hold on the present. With the verb *saillir,* whose vital, eruptive character cannot be translated, Commynes recalls his own projection into mature consciousness: "Near the end of my boy-hood, at the age when horsemanship is first acquired, I was taken to Lille and presented to Duke Charles of Burgundy . . . who took me into his service."[27]

An even more significant (because more voluntary) break with the habits of the past is Commynes's sudden, unexpected desertion of Charles the Bold: "About this time (which was in the year 1472) I entered the service of the king, who had taken most of the servants of his brother."[28] This is an unexpected event only to those readers who have allowed themselves to be lulled to sleep by the apparent monotony of Commynes's account, and have come to think that this historian would allow the past to exercise an iron grip on the present. These quick, arbitrary perforations of the smooth crust of time, though an-nounced brusquely and without previous warning, had long been nurtured during a deceptively silent past, like a calm sea concealing troubled and conflicting currents. None of the chroniclers conveys better than Commynes the notion of a secret past; none is more clearly aware of the necessity of analyzing time past in order to resolve the changes and apparent contradictions of time present. Changes can be analyzed once they have taken place; but they are never predictable.

The Commynian past, however homogeneous, is thus pregnant with the very energies which, if collected at the ripe moment, will enable one to break with continuity. The Commynian character must assume his past, like a responsibility. To accuse the past of paralyzing present action or exercising any deterministic hold whatever on the present can only be an indication of bad faith. Nature in any case is always stronger than discipline or convention; and education can only at best retard the eruption of vital impulse and soften its force. There is in every character a dynamic force that impels him, when the time is ripe, to break with an apparently enslaving past, to act arbitrarily and unpredictably. But if the moment of ripeness is allowed to pass, the unplucked fruit may remain within the organism, to poison the character the rest of his days. Commynes's celebrated remark about the necessity of knowing exactly when to run away from battle seems to apply to any ethical situation whose resolution depends on timely action: "I have seen few people in my life, either here or elsewhere, who knew how to flee at the right time."[29]

Consciousness of self is a prize to be won, sometimes at an astounding price. Few medieval writers are more aware than Commynes that one's irruption into historical awareness entails leaving one's toga of innocence at the gate of a lost paradise. The decision to act historically and to accept the consequences is frequently described as a fall, a loss, an estrangement, a move—whether horizontal or vertical—from an aboriginal source of innocence, happiness, and grace. Commynes's momentous decision to desert Charles of Burgundy in order to enter the service of Louis XI in 1472 was paid with "the losses and afflictions which have befallen me since his death."[30] At Granson in 1476, after the next to last decisive battle of Duke Charles's career, "the duke lost all his most beautiful jewelry, but . . . it was more appropriate to say that he lost honor and possessions that day."[31] The duke's undoing had begun, indeed, at Montlhéry, eleven years earlier, when, after an illusory victory, "God allowed him to fall from the high position he had enjoyed."[32] After his final defeat at Morat, in 1477, Charles "fell into a great illness."[33] After his death, it was the house of Burgundy that fell, and years later its crash could still be heard in the cadences of the Commynian period: "But Our Lord, all of a sudden, caused the fall of this great and sumptuous edifice, this powerful house." The catastrophe is recapitulated a few lines later: "I have seen this house honored on all sides, and then suddenly fallen and turned upside down."[34] And with what appears a coloring of morbid satisfaction, Commynes reflects that the memory of their misfortune will remain with the Burgundians for a long time, or at least the fear of falling again into misfortune.[35]

Commynes's habitual use of leitmotifs such as *perte, fuyte, diminucion* leads one to suggest that he views universal history as undergoing a progressive disintegration, translated by an ever-increasing state of division and pluralization.[36] Such a vision would seem to imply the prior conviction that there once existed a primeval (or prehistorical) state of innocence, grace, and undivided personal and collective energies. For a Christian like Commynes, imbued as he was with an acute sense of guilt (stemming probably from his desertion in 1472), the conviction that "things were better off before" and that man's fallen condition can only inspire a vertiginous sense of vertical procession was simply a matter of course. "Our lifespan is diminished," he reflects ruefully, "and we do not live as long as men did in former times; neither are our bodies as strong, and similarly our faith and loyalty to one another have been weakened."[37]

In both a chronological and an ontological sense, human history proceeds from a higher, anterior source of being. Commynes's universe is a hypostatic one where every phenomenon, including the human one, might be described as a result of procession or dependence. "All men who have ever been famous and have accomplished great deeds have started very young; and that depends on one's education or the grace of God."[38] "I want to point out that he gained great glory and honor in this enterprise; and it came to him solely by the grace of God."[39] "Nothing," Commynes argues, "is effected save by divine disposition: for when princes or kingdoms have enjoyed great prosperity and wealth and disregard the source of such grace ['dont procède telle grace'] God unexpectedly sets an enemy or enemies against them."[40]

In sum, all historical events, especially catastrophic ones such as divine punishment, war, mortality, famine, proceed from "faulte de foy," lack of faith. The Commynian vision of faith extrapolates, outside each personal destiny and outside history at large, an original state of union with the source of grace; lack of faith, which seems responsible for every historical evil ("dont . . . procèdent tous les maux qui sont par le monde") appears to be the initial impulse propelling the individual into history, a psychic birth trauma tearing man from an aboriginal union, forcing him downwards into an awareness of history and flux.[41] He appears to have considered that fall from innocence, that estrangement from the center of grace, not as a prerequisite for man's growing up (a sort of "felix culpa," making history possible) but as its inevitable product, as inseparable from history as is the tree's shadow from the tree. Commynian history is literally a de-cadence, a vertical movement down and away from the center.

Commynes's celebrated aphorism has both a moral and a cosmological significance: "Par *division* se perdent toutes les bonnes choses du monde."[42] In politics as in physics, division is the starting point of disintegration. Perhaps no one better realized the full implication of the aphorism than Commynes's master, Louis XI, who was "more skillful at the art of *separating* people than any other prince I have ever known."[43] In the Commynian chronicle, individuals, like nations, seem to become progressively complicated the older they grow: "When those who should cooperate separate from and abandon each other, it is a sure sign of the destruction of a territory."[44] "I have spoken only of Europe, for I am not well informed of the situation in the other two parts of the world, Asia and Africa; but I have heard that they have as many wars and divisions as we do, and that they are carried on even more mechanically. . . . It may seem, therefore, that these divisions are necessary in all the world which God has given and ordered for every estate and almost for every person."[45]

Distintegration is a monster that feeds upon itself. The more acute the Commynian character's sense of being divided, the more obsessed he is by his need for pluralization. His sense of disintegration increases his appetite for accretion; rather than bring himself together, he accelerates his own dispersion: "Naturally most people are on the lookout for ways to gain advantage [*s'acroistre*] . . . and this danger is especially apparent when princes try to win people over to their side. Although it is not true that "no one has ever gained anything from a fool," a wise prince "works more than any other to gain to his cause any man who could serve him."[46] Louis XI suffered nothing but "travail" from his childhood until his death, like so many other princes "who worked so hard to enrich themselves ['pour se acroistre']." As if they lived in a universe regulated by a malevolent skin of sorrow, Commynes's characters struggle to extend themselves only to discover that their life-span has been conversely shortened: "They worked so hard to enrich themselves ['se acroistre'] and win glory, and suffered so many pains and sorrows and shortened their lives ['et abrégié leur vie']. . . . Would they not have been better off . . . to worry less, to work less, to undertake *fewer* things?"[47]

This final warning, at the end of Book VI, far from being a call to passivity or resignation, is a moral intuition of the highest order: any accretion is an ultimate impoverishment which prolongs man's fallen state and complicates it even further. The more one works "à s'acroistre," the more he extends himself horizontally, the further removed he becomes from the source of his moral energies, the less promising is the prospect of ever collecting his energies. Estrangement from God is ultimately a prevarication against one's own nature, a progressive loosening of the fibers of one's being. In a sentence that could have been written by Plotinus, Commynes considers the "regressus animae" as an effort away from dissolution back toward concentration and firmness: "our only hope should rest in God because He is the source of all our strength and of all goodness, and this is not to be found in anything in this world. But each of us realizes this late in life, after we have been in need of Him. However, it is better late than never."[48]

If the substance of that passage is Plotinian, its conclusion is decidedly Augustinian. Readers of Commynes (and they are many) who are quick to underline the "Machiavellian" or "Pelagian" independence of his thinking disregard, as a rule, such remarks as "chascun de nous la connaist tard," which seems more Augustinian than Pelagian in its echo.[49] While he can in no way be said to be a theologian, Commynes would surely have felt more at home with an Augustine than either a Pelagius or a Machiavelli.

His pessimism as to a man's capacity for self-aggrandizement is, however, the product less of abstract reflection than of bitter experience. Only in prison, smarting over his social and political fall from grace, could Commynes have written: "No matter how wisely men can deliberate on these matters, it is God who concludes things at his own pleasure."[50] That they were conceived in prison weakens neither the truth nor the sincerity of his moral intuitions; as one believes in his sincerity when he implies that a loss of innocence is a necessary byproduct of man's life in history, so one should think him equally sincere when he argues for the necessity of performing a nearly impossible swim against one's personal tide, back toward the source, if one is to avoid total dissolution of energy.[51]

The Commynian character seems afflicted with a sense of diminution that is derived from his dynamic need to look forward in conflict with a residual sense of guilt for having betrayed (or fallen from) the best of his past: youth, innocence, grace. In both a religious and psychological sense, Commynian man is fallen nature: he experiences shame for having grown up, although he could not have grown up without a sense of shame. He has both fallen from a state of innocence and lucidly decided to take the leap. At the core of the Commynian idea of tragedy is an impossible conflict between the dynamic and the static man, between the pragmatist engaged in time and the romantic, nostalgic for a time-less innocence.

The apparently insoluble conflict between static and dynamic man can be dealt with, to Commynes's mind, in two ways. There are mo-ments when he proposes to resolve the conflict by suppressing one of its elements: destroy the dynamic man, he argues, and it follows that the static man will turn his back to the future. He will return to God and to his timeless self. Such is the Commynian idea of conversion: an unconvincing notion, as it is the product not of a redirection of energies but of their failure, their stagnation. "All things considered, our only hope should rest in God."[52] "For in this and similar cases, one's first refuge is to return to God and consider whether one has offended Him in any way, to humble himself before Him, and to acknowledge one's misdeeds."[53] "To speak quite naturally, as an unlettered man with a little experience, would it not be better . . . for all princes and men of moderate social estate . . . to choose the middle road in these mat-ters [of political and personal ambition]? . . . Their lives would be longer, illness would be later in coming, and their deaths, which would be later in coming, would be mourned by more people. Can one find a better example [than Louis XI] to prove that man is worth very little, that this is a brief and miserable life, and that every man, once dead, is as nothing?"[54]

Many of Commynes's readers have questioned the sincerity of those modest proposals to resolve the central conflict of man's existence by negating one of its elements. Whether Commynes himself would have found his religious remedies palatable during his active career is ques-tionable; but he was more receptive to messages of resignation after suffering political disgrace at court and the humiliation of nearly two years in prison.

But a religious conversion is not the only way to deal with the static and dynamic self: Since man is perforce involved in the historical pro-cess yet nostalgic for prehistorical innocence and timeless certitudes, let him practice *saigesse,* the wisdom of the passing moment, an intuition of the truth of things in their state of flux. Commynian *saigesse* seems to differ from *sçavoir* as does Bergsonian intuition from intelligence. *Sçavoir* seems to be that natural sense whose object is either a past his-torical truth or a truth crystallized into timeless mass. Because it is ori-ented toward past, frozen certitudes, *sçavoir* seems a less flexible episte-mological tool than *saigesse.* Its object being a fixed concept, *sçavoir* is a neutral weapon whose effect on historically engaged man depends en-tirely upon the dynamic use he makes of such an object: "A prince or other man of whatever estate he may be, who has power and authority

over others and is well educated, learned, and experienced, will either
be improved as a result, or else made worse: for great *knowledge* [*sçavoir*] makes wicked men worse and good men better. However, it is
probable that knowledge [*sçavoir*] usually does men more good than
harm."[55]

While *sçavoir* is one of the means to express one's nostalgia for espis-
temological fixity, *saigesse* is one's intuition of truth in motion. Commynes uses the word *saige,* or some derivative, nearly two hundred
times in his *Memoirs,* frequently in a morally neutral or even an immoral sense: an indication that he found the word *saige* more adequate
than more static concepts like *sens* or *sçavoir* to convey the notion of
knowledge in action, dynamic intelligence, intuitive cleverness. He dis-
sociates saigesse from its Christian meaning and, in contradistinction to
medieval thinkers before him, ceases to define the term with reference
to objective moral standards.[56] The *saige,* in a Commynian sense, need
not possess predefined and objectively valued virtues (he may or may
not, but his possessing them has nothing to do with his being *saige*);
his is essentially a dynamic, pragmatic, and unpredictable response to
historical change.

But neither religious conversion nor *saigesse* are infallible remedies
to the basic human conflict. If religious conversion is but a means of
denying an inner process whose deteriorative effects have already taken
their toll on the subject, *saigesse* merely retards a deterioration that is
as inevitable as history itself. Every man is doomed to diminution, and
nowhere does Commynes pretend that it can either be avoided or reme-
died. But human disintegration is not a collective event, nor does it
afflict every character in the same way at the same time. If microcosms
fall apart, the center of the macrocosm seems to hold. The universe
seems a closed system with fixed quantities of variously distributed energy. One man's loss is another man's gain: "It is not unusual that after
the decease of so great and powerful a prince great changes would take
place. Some people lose from this, and others gain ['et y ont les ungs
pertes et les autres gaing']. For goods and honors are not divided up
according to the desire of those who request them."[57]

Commynes's final response to the law of the pluralization of matter
is the equally irrefutable law of its conservation. Despite the continual
shuffling and reshuffling of individuals within the Commynian system,
an equilibrating force establishes and maintains a balance among the
actions of individual men and societies. Criminal actions are avenged
by equivalent criminal actions: Charles the Bold is killed at the very
spot where he had ingloriously betrayed a dangerous enemy; the suffer-
ings inflicted by the Spider King on his people must almost mathemati-

cally be cancelled out by the excruciating pain of his final months; and with his tragic death, Charles the Bold has equalized ("fait esgal") the losses and gains of the Burgundian duchy, and his loss yields a sum equal to the felicity of his three forebears.[58]

Equilibrium, like the *diké* of Aeschylean tragedy, rules all collective phenomena. An anticipation of the nineteenth-century idea of the European balance of powers is implicit by extended analogy in one of Commynes's best-known aphorisms: "All things considered, it seems to me that God has created neither man nor beast in this world without establishing some counterpart to oppose him, in order to keep him in humility and fear."[59] On the large balance of political activity, one scale must always present a weight equal to that of the other if political cataclysms are to be avoided. The Flemish city of Ghent provides a counterpoise to the power of the great Burgundian duchy. The ambitions of England are held in check by Scotland, as those of France are tempered by England. Portugal and Spain, Granada and Castille, rival states are paired off everywhere on earth in a manner providentially established, it seems, to serve as goads (*esguillons*) that defy complacency, or as obstacles that arrest ambition. Divisions and rivalries, Commynes reflects, seem to have been established of necessity by God, principally because of the "bestiality" of princes who make ill use of their reason and experience.

If, then, individual characters and nations submit to a historical process of deterioration, corrosion, and pluralization, collectivities are governed by a law of universal equilibrium. Individuals pass while collectivities remain. In an anthropophagous world, princes and subjects devour and are devoured in an endless cycle.

Jean Dufournet has described the greatest of the French medieval chroniclers as a "destroyer of myths." So intense was Commynes's "mauvaise conscience" after his defection from the ranks of Burgundy, argues Dufournet, that his *Memoirs* are a systematic attempt to destroy the assumptions according to which his desertion was immoral or unchivalric.[60]

Must Commynes stand trial as an iconoclast under this, the most somber light ever projected upon him? Or might it not be argued, in turn, that, far from destroying the great chivalric myths, he found them dying around him in the last quarter of the fifteenth century? The foregoing analysis of Commynes's *Memoirs* seems to reveal not a perverse or secret iconoclast, but a fundamentally romantic figure, nostalgic for a past "when things were better off." Might Commynes's bad conscience not be the dissonance within a man whose vision is turned toward the present world of action, while his hearing remains attuned to the echoes of the "hystoires anciennes," not merely those of Joinville's world, but even the innocent "hystoires" of an Edenic past?

A romantic whose mind, despite the modernity of its message, was of an essentially conservative cast, a modern with a backward look, his book, which appears to some like an inventory of destruction, strikes others as a song of lost innocence—the personal innocence of the author and that of an emerging French nation to the collapse of whose feudal institutions he had contributed despite himself. A nation on the threshold of a new era, strengthened and centralized, but at the price of political innocence.

8 CONCLUSION: TWO STYLES

VILLEHARDOUIN considers the act of vision essentially as a process of selection of useful events insofar as they are ordained toward action or the demonstration of a thesis, to the exclusion of details that might serve to complicate, retard, or embarrass the exposition of that thesis. Villehardouin seems to blur or complicate issues consciously for the sole purpose of saving a thesis that he is implicitly trying to uphold, and despite his stated purpose of describing the conquest of Constantinople, the events themselves are subordinated to the thesis and admitted into the chronicler's field of vision only insofar they are in accordance with it.

Joinville's real intention in writing also appears different from his stated one. Written allegedly as a biography of King Louis IX for the edification of his admirers, the *History of Saint Louis* is in fact a book about a class and an institution rather than about a man; insofar as it considers the man it depicts him in his subordination to that institution, whether he lived in accordance with it or exaggerated its canons. Joinville's book is written in demonstration of an implicit thesis, and the details admitted into his field of vision, as well as many of his most significant omissions, are selected in accordance with an ideal and a purpose that transcend the details themselves. In both Villehardouin and Joinville there is a subordination of event to purpose and a consequent dynamism of selection in the act of visual remembrance.

There is no such subordination in Froissart, no distance separating the events from the intention they serve, no hidden thesis, no underlying purpose, no implicit structure. The chronicler's intent is inseparable from the chronicle itself; details are not to be selected or excluded according to whether or not they are in keeping with a transcendent thesis.

117

Since there appears to be no qualitative difference between one event and another, the visual description of each event is to be given a full literary coverage. Each noble enterprise, each feat of arms that has come within the narrator's ken, is to be democratically *enregistré* and kept in perpetual memory.[1] Froissart's is an entirely homogeneous, horizontal world, where every event, including states of consciousness, are smoothly extended as on a horizontal plane. The narration of one event takes up more space than that of another, and therein alone lies the difference between them.

The process is almost, but not quite, the same in the case of the Burgundian chroniclers. Like Froissart they are phenomenalists, in that they do not seem to search for deeper meanings, underlying structures, or transcendent ideals. Like his, their world is a horizontal one, and no rigorous process of selection seems to subordinate one event to the other or all events to an implicit or explicit argument. Yet the visual depiction of events might be described as the penultimate purpose of the chronicle, the ultimate purpose being the literary glory that it reflects upon the chroniclers. Literary glory being proportioned to the "style desservi et requis" (the proper literary style) in which the events are depicted, however, the selection of details cannot be seen as subordinated to an underlying purpose. Rather it can be considered as an end in itself. Events are smoothly and homogeneously exteriorized, since a polished, unbroken narrative is a necessary condition for an artistically valid chronicle. Unlike what is frequently witnessed in Villehardouin and Joinville, no event is set out in relief against another, none enjoys a special validity.

In Basin's chronicle, and again in Commynes's, the historian's vision of details is subservient to an underlying structure implicitly discerned by the chronicler. Basin's vision of man's historical condition is that of a confused musical score to which the historian must provide the key of intelligibility. Some historical events are more important and illustrative of historical intelligibility than others. In its ultimate sense, history is a convergence of temporal and eternal values, each buttressing the other like the ribs of an ogival vault. Commynes, on the other hand, seems to sense beneath the surface of historical events a process of material disintegration, as if the progressive deterioration of the material universe were translated by an ever-increasing pluralization of matter. The process of material disintegration, however, is counterbalanced by a converse process of equilibrium.

As one examines the various visions of historical reality from Villehardouin to Commynes it becomes increasingly clear that the French family of historical writing is composed of two main branches: one might be called the "transcendentalist" and the other the "phenomenalist" branch.

The transcendentalists (Villehardouin, Joinville, Basin, Commynes) have in common a sense of time as duration and development; an underlying, however confused, philosophy of historical process; a wide use of universals and conceptual abstractions; a sense of the complexity of most historical issues and events; a vague or clear sense of a background reality behind the world of appearance. They are generally pessimistic, unworldly but not necessarily otherworldly men who have at some point or other in their lives suffered severe setbacks and humiliations. They are essentially window historians, who consider visual events as a means of seeing through to some inner truth. They have a high sense of interpenetration and confusion, especially of internal images. Their exteriorization of outer images is rarely smooth. Some of their images are brought out into high relief, others are hardly touched upon and sometimes even relegated to the shadows. The transcendentalist never thinks of his work as a literary *oeuvre,* his art is never its own justification. His work is intended to serve a political or moral purpose.

The phenomenalist chronicler (Froissart, Chastellain, La Marche) seems to possess mostly opposite qualities and faults. His is a linear, spatial, mathematical sense of time. His characters rarely develop, rarely age, rarely learn over the years. He has no underlying vision of historical process. He is an implicit nominalist, sensitive to individual detail, accident, outer configuration, rarely to substance and universal knowledge. His general ideas are of a devastating banality. He willfully or unconsciously has little sense of the synthetic picture of the events and issues which he is describing, an amused but naive spectator. He is worldly, optimistic, somewhat venal, implicitly a materialist, in any case not the sort of person who believes in raising theoretical problems. He would rather avoid issues than confront them. He is essentially a mirror historian, in that his vision reflects and is arrested by the event itself. He appears to extend his representations of time, visual detail, or states of consciousness as over a surface. He usually juxtaposes events so as better to understand them. He has a low sense of interpenetration, and simplifies issues in order to avoid confusion. His representation of visual detail is smoothly exteriorized, and he projects a uniform light on all the events of his narrative. He uses neither shadow nor high relief, since he has nothing to prove and nothing to hide. He writes for glory and "gratia artis." He has no moral or political thesis to prove.

Without "twisting" the texts that they might fit prearranged classifications, or forcing one's categories upon them like a mold, one may permissibly argue that the two fundamental ways of viewing historical reality in late medieval France can ultimately be described in terms similar to the "two basic styles" which, according to Eric Auerbach, stand at the root of all Western literary representation: "The two styles, in their opposition, represent basic types: on the one hand, fully externalized description, uniform illumination, uninterrupted connection, free expression, all events in the foreground, displaying unmistakable meanings, few elements of historical development and of psychological perspective; on the other hand, certain parts brought into high relief, others left obscure, abruptness, suggestive influence of the unexpressed, 'background' quality, multiplicity of meanings and the need for interpretation, universal historical claims, development of the concept of the historically becoming, and preoccupation with the problematic."[2] Froissart, Chastellain, and Olivier de la Marche seem adequately to illustrate the former style; Villehardouin, Joinville, Basin, and Commynes are worthy examples of the other.

One might also put to excellent use in differentiating these two families of chroniclers Auerbach's profound distinction between the "legendary" and the "historical" technique. Those I have called phenomenalists make wide use of what Auerbach calls the "legendary" technique. Their accounts run smoothly. "All cross-currents, all friction, all that is casual, secondary to the main event and themes, everything unresolved, truncated and uncertain, which confuses the clear purpose of the action and the simple orientation of the actors, has disappeared."[3] The phenomenalists arrange their material in a simple and straightforward way, detach it from its contemporary historical context, know only clearly outlined men who act from few and simple motives and the continuity of whose feelings and actions remains uninterrupted. The transcendentalists, on the other hand, being historians in a true sense, are more aware of the "various, contradictory, and confused" nature of the historical event. Froissart, Chastellain, and La Marche cultivate the legendary technique almost exclusively; Basin and Commynes are in the full sense historians. Villehardouin, and to a lesser extent Joinville, are historians who make large concessions to the technique of legend.

The greater the writer's historical sense, the further removed he is from any concession to legend, and the more he and his characters are subject to development. Joinville, Basin, and Commynes, and most of their characters, are more fraught with their own biographical past, more distinct as individuals, more vulnerable to the heights and depths of the human experiential process, than are Froissart, Chastellain, La Marche, or any of their hollow, static heroes such as Bascot de Mauléon, Croquart, Charles VI, Philip the Good, and the knights of the Pheasant's Banquet. Such heroes as Gaston de Foix or Duke Philip the

Good, historically real figures to whom their biographers (Froissart and Chastellain) have applied the magic want of legend, are splendidly described, but they undergo no development; they are depicted once and for all; they appear to be always of the same age whenever one sees them; and they never seem to learn.

Not so with Joinville, Saint Louis, Commynes, and Basin. What a difference there is between the Joinville of 1248 who takes leave of his family for the Seventh Crusade, and the Joinville of 1267 who refuses to repeat the same error, or the aged writer of 1309 who dedicates his memoirs to Queen Jeanne of Navarre! What a distance Commynes has traveled, from the young squire of seventeen who arrives at the court of Duke Philip the Good in 1464, and the disenchanted diplomat of 1490 who concedes that "it is better to learn wisdom late than never"! While Chastellain's Duke Philip never seems to age or change, Joinville (despite some concessions to the "legendary" technique of pious hagiography) describes a Saint Louis somewhat mellowed and much chastened as a result of the hapless Seventh Crusade. While Froissart's knights fail to connect one instant of time to another and live from siege to battle and from joust to tournament, Commynes's tragic warrior, Duke Charles the Bold, plunges headlong into the depths of his own willful disintegration. In the historic chronicles of Joinville, Basin, Commynes, even Villehardouin (despite his unfortunate concessions to the "legendary" technique of oversimplification), the old man is more of an individual than the young man; he is more differentiated, more deeply stamped, like a figure on a coin brought into progressively higher relief. Time has worked on him from within, while it has touched the heroes of Froissart, Chastellain, and La Marche from the exterior. While the lives of a Joinville, a Basin, a Commynes, a Louis XI, a Charles the Bold have alternated between success and failure, exaltation and despair, and while their personalities have been deeply modified in the process, Du Guesclin, Charles VI, Gaston de Foix, and Bascot de Mauléon do not seem to have absorbed any of the life to which they have been exposed, as if their chivalric armor were experience-proof.

To pretend that the division of late medieval historiography into two basic styles in France extended the ancient quarrel between nominalists and realists into the historical field would be an oversimplification. The chroniclers discussed here were far removed from the scholastic issue of determining whether universals exist only within the mind. With the exception of clerics like Froissart and Basin, none of them had anything resembling philosophical training, and none seems to have been even remotely aware of the great academic issues and debates of his time. Inasmuch as it can be argued, however, that all men are implicitly either nominalists or realists, the process of polarization which enables one to distinguish the style of a Froissart, a Chastellain, an Olivier de la Marche from that of a Villehardouin, a Joinville, a Basin, a Commynes is not unlike that which enables one to distinguish a realist from a nominalist. At one pole, an overriding interest in the catalogue of concrete singulars, an impatience with issues and theories, a certain gaucheness in handling general ideas; at the other, a relative indifference to the colorful representation of singulars, an implicit conviction that they are the projection of preexisting structures, an instinctive relish for generalizations, for moral issues, for philosophizing. One is temperamentally a nominalist or a realist quite as inescapably as one is melancholic or sanguine.[4]

Curiously enough, those chroniclers for whom history is primarily the pursuit of intelligibility and universal knowledge also seem to have the most highly developed sense of historical development, to be the most acutely aware of history as an unfolding drama. Sensitivity to historical evolution requires quite as much of a philosophical cast of mind as the intuition of essences and metaphysical fixities; and one wonders whether the concept of flux would appear comprehensible to a mind that did not at least implicitly contrast it with the concept of staticity. From the Presocratics to Aristotle, unity and multiplicity, substance and flux are found to coexist with ease within the same philosophical systems. It is hardly a paradox, therefore, that the most conceptually oriented of the chroniclers should also be the most sensitive to change, evolution, disintegration.

It is noteworthy, finally, that the rise of a rather mature historical sense in late fifteenth-century France and the gradual disappearance of the "legendary" technique in historical writing seems to coincide fully with the decline of the myth of chivalry. In his study of the transformations of that medieval institution, R. L. Kilgour described the ages of chivalry as "the age of superiority, the age of privilege, and the age of vanity. Its first and heroic age achieved the amazing fusion of military glory with religious fervor. With the gradual weakening of the great motive forces chivalry was content to rest upon its laurels, elaborating its standards of courtesy and gallantry. The final period shows us a chivalry bent on mad, exaggerated display, as if to hide its impotence and its sordid vices under gilded armor and flowered silk."[5]

Villehardouin and Joinville, writing in an "age of superiority" when chivalry had a religious and historical *raison d'etre,* wrote of it as historians paying occasional lip-service to the legendary techniques of epic and romance. During the "age of privilege," with the gradual weakening of its great motive forces, chivalry is as much a subject matter for legend as for history; and in Froissart the distinction between history and legend is blurred. It tends to disappear entirely with the Burgundian chroniclers, who seem to portray history as legend gone wild.

Basin and Commynes belong to what might already be considered the "post-chivalric age." Their lucidity is equal to their sense of boredom; they are conscious of the multifaceted nature of their period; they are no longer impressed by the chivalric anachronisms of former masters and patrons who are not living with their time. By the end of the fifteenth century, a clear, permanent line circumscribes the respective domains of history and legend. Chivalric deeds are relegated forever to the realm of romance; and history is henceforth considered as a confused, inglorious battlefield, where honor cannot be distinguished from victory. In Commynes's phrase, "Ceux qui gaignent en ont toujours l'honneur."

NOTES TO THE CHAPTERS

1 THE DISINTEGRATION OF SYSTEMS

1. For a fuller discussion of the various historical schemes used by the Church Fathers, see my article, "The Ages of Man and the Ages of the World," *Revue des Etudes Augustiniennes* XI, 3–4 (1966):193–202.

2. On this point see R. Hanning, *The Vision of History in Early Britain* (New York: Columbia University Press, 1966), p. 29.

3. Eusebius, *The History of the Church from Christ to Constantine,* translated with an Introduction by G. H. Williamson (New York: New York University Press, 1966), p. 31.

4. Augustine, *De Genesi contra Manichaeos,* in Migne, *Patrologia Latina,* 34, cols. 190–93. The treatise, written some time between A.D. 388 and 390, was intended to refute a literal, anthropomorphic interpretation of Genesis taught by the Manichaeans. The *De Genesi* contains Augustine's longest development of the analogy between the ages of man and the ages of the world. The analogy is also developed in the *De Civitate Dei,* Bk. X, Ch. 14, and Bk. XVI, Ch. 43, part 3.

5. Although the medieval tradition of universal chronicle writing survived until the seventeenth century, it was already dying by the start of the fourteenth. In this regard it is noteworthy that Agrippa d'Aubigné's *Histoire universelle,* written in the late sixteenth century, should in fact be a detailed record not of the history of salvation "from Adam to the present" (as would have been the case as late as Vincent of Beauvais), but of the history of France between 1553 and 1602. One of the last historians in the West to attempt a universal history within the literal limits of the Eusebian and Augustinian chronological systems was Bossuet. His *Discours sur l'histoire universelle* begins with the Creation; history is divided into seven ages; the events of Judaeo-Christian history and those of the great pagan empires progress along parallel lines, as in Eusebius. In a style that often reads like a French translation of Augustine, Bossuet attempts a synthesis of all ancient history, secular and religious, in demonstration of his prefatory

thesis that the empires of this world have their rise and fall, but that the history of the revelation of God endures forever. Bossuet's universal chronicle, written in conscious imitation of "the chronologists" who spoke of "the world's duration in seven ages," was perhaps the last example of its kind in Western historiographical literature. It brought the waning tradition of universal chronicle writing to a magnificent though anticlimatic close. The *Discours sur l'histoire universelle* reads like an exquisite funeral oration, pronounced over the winding sheet of an ancient king.

6. A. A. Vasiliev, *History of the Byzantine Empire, 1324–1453* (Madison: University of Wisconsin Press, 1952), II, 452.

7. Two and a half centuries later, at the Pheasant's Banquet held at Lille in February 1454, the knights and lords of the Order of the Golden Fleece, in the wake of the Burgundian duke, Philip the Good, were to vow, in a setting far more decorous and worldly than that of Ecri, to fight for the recovery of Constantinople from the Turks. But they were never to go. Between 1200 and 1450, European chivalry had declined in its fervor. The French barons of Ecri may have taken their vow in playful surroundings, but they carried it out; and the motives for their going were essentially religious. They had something of the courtliness and much of the bravado that were so to characterize their Burgundian descendants, but they knew that a vow was meaningless if unexecuted.

8. E. Lavisse, *Histoire de France* (Paris: Hachette, 1911), III, Part I, 383 (hereafter cited as "Lavisse").

9. Vasiliev, *History of the Byzantine Empire,* II, 453–54.

10. Ibid., pp. 454–55.

11. Ibid., pp. 452–53.

12. Ibid., p. 460.

13. Ibid., p. 464.

14. Ibid., p. 456.

15. Rutebeuf, "Les Ordres de Paris," *Oeuvres complètes de Rutebeuf,* edited by E. Faral and J. Bastin (Paris: A. et J. Picard, 1959–60), I, 323.

16. Lavisse, II, Part II, 321.

17. Rutebeuf, "Renart le Bestourné," *Oeuvres complètes,* I, 539.

18. Lavisse, III, Part II, 249.

19. William of Ockham (b. ca. 1290, d. ca. 1349), an Oxford Franciscan, is considered the founder of the most radical form of fourteenth-century nominalism. Ockham argued that universal concepts (e.g., man), unlike singular concepts (e.g., this man, John) have strictly no foundation in any reality outside the mind. Universal concepts are merely mental signs (*nomina*) that designate an outward resemblance between particulars (e.g., *this* man and *that* man), but they predicate no real essence that is common to each of the particulars. Among the logical consequences of Ockhamist nominalism are: the fragmentation of the universe into isolated, individual objects (the only possible science is the science of particulars); the illusory nature of metaphysics; and the undemonstrability of matters of faith traditionally considered as accessible to reason (e.g., the existence of God, the immortality of the soul).

20. For these ideas I am indebted to Daniel Poirion, *Le Poète et le prince* (Paris: Presses Universitaires de France, 1965), pp. 63, 89–90.

21. *The Chronicle of Jean de Venette,* edited with an Introduction and Notes by R. A. Newhall (New York: Columbia University Press, 1953), p. 63.

22. Ibid., p. 66.

23. *Homo Ludens,* p. 220, as quoted in Poirion, *Le Poète et le prince,* p. 98.

24. Ibid.

25. Philippe de Commynes, *The Memoirs,* edited by S. Kinser, with a translation by I. Cazeaux (Columbia, S. C.: University of South Carolina Press, 1969), p. 353.

26. Thomas Basin, *Histoire de Louis XI,* edited by Charles Samaran (Paris: Les Belles Lettres, 1963–66), I, 19–21.

27. John Fortescue, *Governance of England,* edited by C. Plummer (Oxford: Clarendon Press, 1885), as cited in Lavisse, IV, Part II, 129.

28. Lavisse, IV, Part II, 294–96.

29. Commynes, *The Memoirs,* p. 355.

2 VILLEHARDOUIN: HISTORY IN BLACK AND WHITE

1. Textual references are to G. de Villehardouin, *La Conquête de Constantinople,* edited by E. Faral (Paris: Les Belles Lettres, 1938). Biographical material on Villehardouin has been taken from R. Bossuat, art., "Geoffroi de Villehardouin," *Dictionnaire des lettres francaises* (Paris: A Fayard, 1964), pp. 304–307.

2. For a discussion of the problem of Villehardouin's sincerity, see Villehardouin, *La Conquête,* I, xvi–xxxvii; D. E. Queller and S. J. Stratton, "A Century of Controversy on the Fourth Crusade," in *Studies in Medieval and Renaissance History,* edited by William M. Bowsky (Lincoln: University of Nebraska Press, 1969), VI, 235–77.

3. Robert de Clari, *De chiaus qui conquistrent Constantinople,* edited by Philippe Lauer (Paris: H. Champion, 1924). Biographical material on Robert has been taken from U. T. Holmes, art., "Robert de Clari," *Dictionnaire des lettres francaises, Le Moyen âge,* p. 639.

4. For a summary of the controversy on the origins of the Fourth Crusade, see Queller and Stratton, "A Century of Controversy on the Fourth Crusade," in *Studies in Medieval and Renaissance History,* edited by Bowsky, 233–77. I have used M. R. B. Shaw's translation of Villehardouin, *Joinville and Villehardouin: Chronicles of the Crusades* (London: Penguin Books, 1963), and E. H. McNeal's edition and translation of Robert de Clari, *The Conquest of Constantinople* (New York: Columbia University Press, 1939). Whenever I have disagreed with these translations I have provided my own. On Villehardouin's habit of dividing the world into opposite camps, see *La Conquête,* I, par. 86, 87, 100, 234, 236.

5. A. Pauphilet, *Le Legs du moyen âge* (Melun: d'Argences, 1950), p. 219.

6. *La Conquête,* I, par. 2.

7. Ibid., par. 11.

8. Ibid., par. 14.

9. Ibid., par. 18.

10. Ibid.

11. Ibid., par. 25.

12. The one adjective of color that retains his attention is the *vermilion* of the Byzantine emperor's boots (ibid., par. 227, and again par. 245).

13. Ibid., par. 27–29.

14. Ibid., par. 57.

15. Ibid., par. 60.

16. E.g., ibid., par. 61: "Those who had retained their possessions were highly delighted and refused to add anything of their own, since they were now quite confident that the army would be broken up and the troops dispersed. But God . . . was not willing for this to happen."

17. Ibid., par. 100.

18. Ibid., par. 77: "Comment porroit estre prise tel ville par force, se Diex meïsmes nel fait?"

19. Ibid., par. 105.

20. Ibid., par. 108.

21. Ibid., par. 110.

22. Ibid., par. 93.

23. Ibid., par. 95–97.

24. Ibid.

25. Villehardouin's clever game of obfuscation has succeeded down to the present. In his Introduction to *La Conquête,* I, xxii, Faral argues that the refusal of the Abbot of Vaux and Simon de Montfort to attack Constantinople did not prevent them, several years later, from destroying the Albigensians, "des hérétiques, mais pourtant des chrétiens." The point at issue is not whether the dissenters were contradictory in their conduct. One might simply remark that not unlike Villehardouin, Faral almost succeeds in distracting the reader's attention from the event at hand toward an ulterior and unrelated event.

26. Ibid., par. 99. Villehardouin attempts further to blur the embarrassing central issue by narrating it in an impersonal style as if it had been witnessed by someone else: "And the book says that there were only 12 who took the oath."

27. Ibid., par. 101.

28. Ibid., par. 116–17.

29. Robert de Clari, *The Conquest of Constantinople,* translated by E. H. McNeal (New York: Columbia University Press, 1939), pp. 59–66.

30. *La Conquête,* I, par. 120.

31. Robert de Clari, *La Conquête de Constantinople,* edited by Ph. Lauer (Paris, 1924), ch. XIII (my translation).

32. *La Conquête,* I, par. 122.

33. Ibid.: "Et por ce dit hom que de mil males voies puet on retorner."

34. Ibid., par. 128.

35. Ibid., par. 162.

36. Ibid., par. 204.

37. Ibid., II, par. 218.

38. Ibid., II, par. 249–51.

39. Nicetas Choniates, *Devastatio,* quoted in E. Pears, *The Fall of Constantinople* (New York, 1886), pp. 354–55.

40. *La Conquête,* II, par. 253. One should note the Manichaean language of Villehardouin's text: "Li uns aporta *bien* et li autres *mauvaisement.*" Robert de Clari gives a less biased account of the event: "Afterwards it was ordered that all the wealth of the spoils should be brought to a certain church in the city. The wealth was brought there, and they took ten knights, high men, of the pilgrims, and ten of the Venetians who were thought to be honorable, and set them to guard the wealth. . . . And each one of the rich men took gold ornaments or cloth of silk and gold or anything else he wanted and carried it off. So in this way they began to rob the treasure, so that nothing was shared with the common people of the host or the poor knights or the sergeants who had helped to win the treasure" (McNeal translation, pp. 101–102).

41. *La Conquête,* II, par. 256–500.

42. Pauphilet, *Le Legs,* p. 95.

43. C. A. Sainte-Beuve, "G. de Villehardouin," *Causeries du lundi,* 6 février 1854, p. 412. Sainte-Beuve's portrait of Villehardouin ends on a dithyrambic note: "He has tears of pity beneath his visor, but he does not overuse them. He can get down on both knees, and without weakness, get up on his feet again. His even temper and his common sense are equal to the situations in which he finds himself. In the breach to the very end of the battle, he carries his sword intrepidly and his pen simply. Among historians who also qualify as men of action, he is one of the most honorable and complete of his time."

44. *La Conquête,* I, xxx–xxxvii: "He was a lord. He belonged to the order of chivalry whose law was composed of two commandments: be faithful and be brave."

3   JOINVILLE: HISTORY AS CHIVALRIC CODE

1. Some biographical material on Joinville has been gathered from R. Bossuat, art., "Jean de Joinville," *Dictionnaire des lettres francaises: le moyen âge* (Paris: A. Fayard, 1964), pp. 417–19.

2. On August 6, 1297, Pope Boniface VIII summarized the canonization process of King Louis IX, begun in 1273, by saying that the last inquest alone had necessitated "more documents than an ass could carry." During the canonization process, all persons who had known Louis IX closely were invited to give their testimony. The written record of much of this testimony has been lost. However, two biographers, besides Joinville, expanded their testimony in the form of written memoirs: Geoffroi de Beaulieu, Saint Louis's confessor; and Guillaume de Chartres, his chaplain. Between December 1302 and October 1303, Guillaume de Saint Pathus, who had been confessor to Queen Marguerite (Saint Louis's wife)

for eighteen years, summarized most of the canonization testimony in a later biography of the king, translated into French as *Vie Monseigneur saint Loys,* ed. by Delaborde in 1899. These three pious biographies of Saint Louis contain some interesting materials; but on the whole they make for tedious reading and fail to achieve their edifying purpose.

3. John of Joinville, *The Life of Saint Louis,* translated by René Hague (London: Sheed and Ward, 1955), p. 26. Unless otherwise specified, all translated quotations from Joinville's text are taken from this source. References are cited in the text. For references to the original I have used Natalis de Wailly's edition of the *Histoire de Saint Louis* (Paris, 1874; reprinted in 1965 by the Johnson Reprint Corporation).

4. On this point, see Joan Evans' excellent introduction to her *History of Saint Louis* (Oxford: Oxford University Press, 1938), pp. xiii–xxviii, esp. pp. xxi–xxii.

5. Ibid., p. xx.

6. *The Life of Saint Louis,* p. 7.

7. Ibid., XXXVI, 171: "The common folk took up with loose women, for which . . . the King dismissed many of them. I asked him why he had done so."

8. See esp. Chapters XIII and CXXV.

9. *Life,* XCIX, 505: "The Knight chose to forfeit his horse and left the camp."

10. *Life,* CXXXVIII, 685. Joinville, who did not witness this incident and is somewhat reserved about telling it, derived this piece of information from Guillaume de Saint Pathus. In his biography of the king, this obsequious confessor of Queen Marguerite (the King's wife) applauds the king's zeal in this matter. Pope Clement IV had issued a bull in 1268 asking for moderation in punishing such offenders (according to Hague, *The Life of Saint Louis,* p. 293). Louis IX was literally trying to be *plus catholique que le pape.*

11. On the concept of tripartite society in medieval Europe, see Jacques Le Goff, *La Civilisation de l'occident médiéval* (Paris: Arthaud, 1965), ch. 5; W. J. Sedgefield, *King Alfred's Old English Version of Boethius* (Oxford: Clarendon Press, 1899); J. M. Wallace-Hadrill, *Early Germanic Kingship in England and on the Continent* (Oxford: Clarendon Press, 1971), ch. 6.

12. On *preudome* and *preudomie,* see A. R. Boysen, *Ueber den Begriff preu im Französischen (preu, prou, prouesse, prud'homme, prude, pruderie),* Inaugural-Dissertation, Westfälische Wilhelms-Universität zu Munster, Lengerich, 1941; G. S. Burgess, *Contributions à l'étude du vocabulaire pré-courtois,* Publications Romanes et Francaises, 110 (Geneva: Droz, 1970); *Speculum* XLVI (1971): 363–64.

13. Aristotle, *Nicomachean Ethics,* 1123 b, in Richard McKeon, ed., *The Basic Works of Aristotle* (New York: Random House, 1941), p. 992.

14. *The History of Saint Louis,* p. xxiii. Joan Evans uses the modern French spelling of *prud'homme.* I have employed Joinville's spelling throughout.

15. I have translated the phrase myself, since René Hague does not specifically translate the word *renommée.*

16. This point is well taken by Evans, *The History of Saint Louis,* p. xxiii. In the original text the word *preudome* refers to someone with or above the rank

of knight. (See de Wailly, *Histoire de Saint Louis,* p. 367, under the word *Preudom.*) On one occasion, however, Joinville uses the expression *cis preudom* of a greyfriar of extraordinary spiritual and humane qualities (de Wailly, *Histoire,* section 38d).

17. *Life,* LXIV, 324: "I sent for my people and told them I was a dead man, for I had a tumour in my throat. They asked me how I knew, and I showed them; as soon as they saw the water pouring out of my throat and nostrils they began to weep."

18. Here I disagree with Evans, *The History of Saint Louis,* p. xxiv: "It is with a conscious joy that he recounts the few occasions when Saint Louis acted rather as *prud'homme* than *dévot.*" I believe Joinville considered Louis's lapses into excessive piety as exceptional deviations from his usual *preudomie.*

19. *Life,* LXIII, 318–19: The storekeeper advises Joinville and his men to surrender to the Saracens on land rather than to the Sultan's galleys on the Nile, as the Saracens are sure to kill them or sell them to the Bedouins. "We paid no attention," comments Joinville, and the matter ends there.

20. Such, in substance, is the attitude shared by Sainte-Beuve, Joan Evans, Paul Guth, and other critics, although it has admittedly not been expressed in precisely these terms.

21. For the text of Joinville's *Credo,* see Hague, *The Life of Saint Louis,* pp. 223–37.

22. As quoted by Paul Tillich in *The New Being* (New York: Scribners, 1955), p. 142.

4 FROISSART: HISTORY AS SURFACE

1. Biographical material on Froissart has been gathered from F. L. Ganshof, art., "Jean Froissart," *Dictionnaire des lettres francaises, le moyen âge* (Paris: A. Fayard, 1964), pp. 411–14, and from Kervyn de Lettenhove, ed., *Oeuvres de Froissart* (Brussels: V. Devaux, 1867–77), I.

2. The first edition of Froissart's *Chroniques* (Paris: Le Noir, 1505) was entitled *Le premier volume de Froissart des Croniques de France, d'Engleterre, d'Escoce, d'Espaigne, de Bretaigne, de Gascongne, de Flandres et lieux circonvoisins.*

3. F. L. Ganshof, "Jean Froissart," *Dictionnaire des lettres francaises,* 413. Cf. Auguste Molinier, *Les Sources de l'histoire de France,* IV, *Les Valois,* 1328–1461 (Paris: A. Picard, 1904), pp. 13–14: "Enfin il n'a vu que le côté extérieur des choses . . . ; il n'a du monde de son temps qu'une idée *superficielle.* . . . Ce n'est ni un penseur, ni un politique, ni même une âme passionnée."

4. Textual references in this chapter will be to Jean Froissart, *Chroniques,* ed. by Kervyn de Lettenhove (Brussels: V. Devaux, 1867–77), 25 vols. English translations of the text are my own.

5. Joinville, *Histoire de Saint Louis,* edited by N. De Wailly (Paris, 1874), Ch. 28; Villehardouin, *La Conquête de Constantinople,* edited by E. Faral (Paris: Les Belles Lettres, 1938–39), I, Ch. 25.

6. Froissart, *Chroniques,* XI, 17.

7. Ibid., p. 36.

8. Ibid.: "At an arrow's distance from the town, there is a pass called the Watch. A tower is built over the road, between the cliff and the river. Beneath the tower, over the pass, an iron door can be raised and lowered. Six persons might hold off this pass against an army. The rocks and the river make it impossible for more than two to ride abreast."

9. Ibid., XIV, 15–16. If, on the other hand, the number and the position of objects within a determined space remain fixed (e.g., the disguised "angels" in the makeshift sky above the Saint Denis gate, symbolizing fixed stars), the visual impression is one of order and harmony (p. 8).

10. Ibid., pp. 8–13.

11. Ibid., p. 10.

12. Ibid., XV, 84–90. On the different conceptions of the "savage" in the Middle Ages, see Richard Bernheimer, *Wild Men in the Middle Ages: A Study in Art, Sentiment, and Demonology* (Cambridge, Mass.: Harvard University Press, 1953).

13. *Chroniques,* XI, 64.

14. Ibid., p. 65.

15. Ibid., XIV, 217.

16. Ibid.

17. Ibid., XI, 86.

18. Ibid., p. 87.

19. Ibid., pp. 87–88.

20. Ibid., pp. 99–100.

21. Ibid., p. 100.

22. Ibid., XIV, 321–22.

23. Ibid., XV, 35–53.

24. Ibid., pp. 40–41.

25. Ibid., p. 41. Similarly, when the count of Armagnac goes mad after a sunstroke (*Chroniques,* XIV, 308), he no longer feels retained in a specific *locus,* but experiences the familiar, delirious sensation of travelling through space: "Si luy fut advis que il fuist en paradis."

26. Ibid., XV, 47.

27. Ibid., XI, 74.

28. Montaigne, *Essais,* II, quoted by Georges Poulet, *Etudes sur le temps humain* (Paris: Plon, 1949), I, 1.

29. *Chroniques,* XI, 70–71.

30. Whereas Froissart's interviews provide a cumulative, arithmetical progression of units of information, his account of some other events follows a geometric pattern. The explosion of the peasant Jacquerie revolt, for example, is an expansion of concentric circles that seems to function according to a secret coefficient. The progression of the revolt, at its inception, is arithmetical and as easy to localize as points along a line: "Soon after the delivery of the king of Navarre, there occurred a great, awe-inspiring turmoil in several parts of the French kingdom, such as in Beauvoisin, in Brie, along the Marne, in the regions

of Valois and Coucy, and around Soissons. A few peasants from the neighboring villages assembled in Beauvoisin. At first they were no more than a hundred. Armed with nothing more than knives and irontipped sticks, they marched on the home of a neighboring knight, broke into the house, killed the knight, his wife, and all of his children, and burned the house down. Next, they broke into another castle and did worse. . . . They did the same thing in several castles and respectable homes" (ibid., VI, 44–45).

When the "Jacques" begin to multiply and spread concentrically, however, their activities reach the point of ubiquity: "They multiplied to such an extent that they soon numbered six thousand; and everywhere they went, their numbers grew" (ibid., p. 46).

31. Ibid., II, 4.

32. Ibid., VII, 428.

33. Ibid., XIII, 247 (on the victory of the Scots over the English at the battle of Otterburn): "Ainsi vont les choses: ceulx qui ont eu dommage, se plaignent, et ceulx qui ont fait profit à quoyque ce soit, jouissent."

34. Ibid., XIV, 33 (on the progressive disenchantment of the court of Charles VI with the charming duke of Ireland): "Or n'est-il rieus dont on ne se tanne."

35. Ibid., p. 206 (on Aymerigot Marcel's violent death): "Ainsi paye fortune ses gens: quant elle les a eslevés tout hault sur la roe, elle les reverse tout bas en la boe."

36. E.g., F. S. Shears, *Froissart, Chronicler and Poet* (London: G. Routledge and Sons, 1930), pp. 110–24.

37. See esp. Georges Poulet, *L'Espace proustien* (Paris: Gallimard, 1959), pp. 58–59.

38. *Chroniques*, XVII, 539–40 (the duke of Anjou and Robert Knowles during the siege of Derval).

39. Ibid., XIV, 80.

40. Compare, for example, Froissart's description of the jousts in London (ibid., XIV, 253–69) with his account of the battle of Cocherel (VI, 411–46).

41. Ibid., XI, 107–29.

42. Ibid., p. 119: "Si ay-je tenu frontière et fait guerre pour le roy d'Angleterre, car mon héritaige siet en Bourdellois."

5 CHASTELLAIN AND LA MARCHE: HISTORY AS NARCISSISM

1. Enguerrand de Monstrelet, a native Picard, was chronologically the first of such historiographers. His two books of *Chronicles*, written as a sequel to Froissart's, deal with events in France and Burgundy from 1400 to 1444. Like all fifteenth-century Burgundian chroniclers, Monstrelet considered Froissart as his model, but he lacked both Froissart's readable style and wide experience. Monstrelet's official successor was Matthieu d'Escouchy, who pursued Monstrelet's

chronicle from 1444 until 1461. Other Burgundian *minores* include Le Fèvre de Saint Rémy, Jean de Troyes, Jean Molinet, and Jean de Wavrin.

2. Biographical information on the Burgundian chroniclers has been taken from A Molinier, *Les Sources de l'histoire de France*, IV, *Les Valois* (Paris, 1904); J. Calmette, *Les Grands ducs de Bourgogne* (Paris: A. Michel, 1949), pp. 265–68; J. A. C. Buchon, ed., *Oeuvres historiques inédites de G. Chastellain* (Paris: Desrez, 1883), "Notice" pp. 1–lixiii; H. Beaune and J. d'Arbaumont, eds., *Mémoires d'Olivier de la Marche* (Paris: H. Loones, 1883–88), IV, i–xc.

3. Calmette, *Les Grands ducs de Bourgogne*, p. 263.

4. Unless otherwise indicated, references to Chastellain's works and all titles are to Buchon, *Oeuvres historiques*. Citations from Olivier de la Marche are taken from Beaune and d'Arbaumont, *Mémoires d'Olivier de la Marche*.

5. Chastellain, *Chronique du duc Philippe*, in *Oeuvres historiques*, pp. 1–5.

6. Chastellain, *Chronique des ducs de Bourgogne*, in *Oeuvres historiques*, p. 390.

7. Chastellain, *Exposition sur vérité mal prise*, p. 529.

8. *Mémoires d'Olivier de la Marche*, Prologue, I, 10.

9. Ibid., I, 95–96.

10. Chastellain, *Chronique des ducs de Bourgogne*, p. 143.

11. Chastellain, *Eloge du bon duc Philippe*, in *Oeuvres historiques*, p. 505.

12. *Mémoires d'Olivier de la Marche*, I, 10–12.

13. E.g., the funeral of Duke Philip the Good (ibid., III, 60): "Et pour monstrer et donner à entendre les seremonies et les pompes qui furent tenues . . . et puis si grant nombre de chevaliers, escuyers et nobles hommes, *que c'estoit belle chose à les veoir*" (italics added).

14. Ibid., II, 422.

15. Ibid., p. 242: "une noblesse si bien eccoustrée de pompes et d'abillements, que c'estoit belle chose à veoir."

16. Chastellain, *Eloge du duc Charles le Hardi* in *Oeuvres historiques*, p. 509; "descrire et peindre pour tout temps futur et présent."

17. Chastellain, *Eloge du bon duc Philippe*, pp. 503–05.

18. Chastellain, *Chronique des ducs de Bourgogne*, p. 113.

19. Ibid., p. 118.

20. *Mémoires d'Olivier de la Marche*, III, 108–109.

21. Chastellain, *Eloge du bon duc Philippe*, p. 506.

22. Chastellain, *Chronique des ducs de Bourgogne*, p. 391.

23. Ibid., p. 401.

24. Cf. Chastellain's Prologue to his *Chronique du duc Philippe*, reviewing the succession of worldly empires from the first day of creation until the year 1453: Hebrew, Macedonian, Trojan, Roman, French ("miroir aux verteux").

25. Chastellain, *Chronique des ducs de Bourgogne*, p. 112.

26. *Livre des faits de messire Jacques de Lalaing*, Chapter VII, cited in Beaune and d'Arbaumont, *Mémoires d'Olivier de la Marche*, IV, xxvii.

27. *Mémoires d'Olivier de la Marche*, II, 340–91. Cf. Calmette, *Les Grands ducs de Bourgogne*, p. 307. On the elephant and castle, see W. S. Heckscher,

"Bernini's Elephant and Obelisk," *Art Bulletin* XXIX (1947):158–65. For additional bibliography, see Gérard Brault, *Early Blazon: Heraldic Terminology in the Twelfth and Thirteenth Centuries with Special Reference to Arthurian Literature* (Oxford: Clarendon Press, 1972), p. 248.

28. *Mémoires d'Olivier de la Marche,* II, 367.

29. Ibid., pp. 381–82.

30. Ibid., p. 385, a vow taken by Monseigneur de Charny.

31. It should be noted, however, that this sort of vow is also part of a long tradition and even engendered a literary genre: *Voeux du paon, Voeux de l'épervier, Voeux du heron,* etc.; see Brault, *Early Blazon,* pp. 146–47.

32. Chastellain, *Exposition sur vérité mal prise,* pp. 510–12.

33. *Mémoires d'Olivier de la Marche,* I, 14.

34. Ibid., p. 184.

35. Chastellain, *Chronique des ducs de Bourgogne,* pp. 124–26.

36. Chastellain, *Chronique du duc Philippe,* p. 14–22.

37. Ibid., p. 26.

38. *Eloge du bon duc Philippe,* pp. 505–506.

39. Chastellain, *Chronique du duc Philippe,* p. 23.

40. Both texts are taken from Georges Doutrepont, *La Littérature francaise à la cour des ducs de Bourgogne* (Paris: H. Champion, 1909), pp. 467–68.

41. For Olivier's references to Chastellain as "perle et estoille," and to his "subtil parler," see *Mémoires d'Olivier de la Marche,* I, 14, 184. Chastellain's contemporaries "hardly knew his chronicles which had remained unfinished, and praised above all some rather declamatory opuscules and some rather diffuse verse. . . . After his death, historians cited only rare fragments of his works" (de Lettenhove, *Oeuvres de Georges Chastellain,* I, vii). Chastellain's reputation as a subtle talker was based, then, on the recitation of some of his poems and "opuscules déclamatoires." Fragments of his *Chronicles* may have numbered among those "opuscules" which were recited at court.

42. *Chronique du duc Philippe,* p. 112.

43. Ibid., p. 20.

44. Ibid., p. 63.

45. *Chronique des ducs de Bourgogne,* pp. 147–48.

46. *Exposition sur vérité mal prise,* p. 529.

47. Isidore of Seville, *Etymologiae,* I, 40–43, VIII, 7, cited in W. J. S. Sayers, "The Beginnings and Early Development of Old French Historiography," Ph.D. dissertation, Columbia University, 1966, p. 36. I am indebted to Sayers' informative thesis, especially pp. 15–38.

48. Chastellain, *Exposition,* p. 529.

49. *Mémoires d'Olivier de la Marche,* I, 13. Cf. p. 187.

50. Cicero, *De Legibus,* I, 5, quoted in Sayers, "The Beginnings and Early Development of Old French Historiography," p. 19.

51. Chastellain, *Chronique du duc Philippe,* p. 4.

52. Chastellain, *Chronique des ducs de Bourgogne,* p. 127.

53. *Eloge du bon duc Philippe,* pp. 505, 509.

6   BASIN: HISTORY *Cum Ira et Studio*

1. The following biographical material is taken from Thomas Basin, *Histoire des règnes de Charles VII et de Louis XI,* edited by J. Quicherat (Paris: J. Renouard, 1855–59), I, lxxxix sq. (cited hereafter as Quicherat).

2. D. B. Wyndham Lewis, *King Spider* (New York: Coward-McCann, 1929), p. 410. This quotation from Lewis' popular life of Louis XI is taken from a chapter on the life of Thomas Basin.

3. Quicherat, I, 76.

4. Quicherat is perhaps wrong on one point, at least: a lively imagination does not necessarily detract from a chronicler's lucidity. Uncommitted historians are not always the least muddled, nor do partisan historians always permit anger to blur their vision. The simple clarity of Villehardouin's chronicle is a direct result of his being partisan; and Chastellain's almost morbid fear of partiality adds neither logic nor conciseness to his life of Philippe le Bon. Basin remains aware of the complexity of historical events despite his partiality toward some of their protagonists, and he usually manages to draw back to the distance that allows him best to focus his vision.

5. Thomas Basin, *Histoire de Charles VII,* edited by Charles Samaran (Paris: Les Belles Lettres, 1933–44), II, 308–10. Unless otherwise indicated, all subsequent references will be to this edition of the text. All English translations are mine.

6. T. Basin, *Histoire de Louis XI,* edited by Charles Samaran (Paris: Les Belles Lettres, 1963), I, 295.

7. The moral and political intentions of the "coalition for the public weal" are discussed in ibid., I, 171–85. The battle of Montlhéry is dealt with in one paragraph, ibid., p. 195.

8. Ibid., pp. 303–305: "Ce traité comprit donc de nombreux articles, par lesquels le roi promettait au duc de Bourgogne qu'il ferait et accomplirait beaucoup de choses."

9. Ibid., p. 3.

10. Ibid., pp. 3–5.

11. *Histoire de Charles VII,* II, 37–38; cf. I, 7.

12. Ibid., I, Book II, Chapters IX–XVI.

13. Ibid., pp. 155–57.

14. Ibid., II, 265–68.

15. E.g., *Histoire de Louis XI,* p. 335, where King Louis XI suddenly becomes aware of the way he has been conducting himself: "Time can also heal stubborn hatreds" (p. 343).

16. *Histoire de Charles VII,* I, 40–42.

17. King Henry's speech has much the same movement and even some of the phrasing as Catiline's before his final battle, in Sallust, *De Coniuratione Catilinae,* LVII, in *Salluste,* edited by A. Ernout (Paris: Les Belles Lettres, 1946), pp.

119–21. See P. Archambault, "Sallust in France," *Papers on Language and Literature* VI (Summer 1968):245–46.

18. *Histoire de Charles VII*, II, 186.

19. Ibid., I, 82–84.

20. *Histoire de Louis XI*, pp. 145–47. Basin constantly records motives. To him, states of consciousness are as historically real as are actions.

21. E.g., *Histoire de Charles VII*, II, 266; cf. *Histoire de Louis XI*, I, 147–49.

22. *Histoire de Louis XI*, I, 193–95; but cf. Commynes, *The Memoirs*, edited by S. Kinser and I. Cazeaux (Columbia, S.C.: University of South Carolina Press, 1969), pp. 109–15.

23. *Histoire de Louis XI*, I, 303–305; cf. Commynes, *The Memoirs*, esp. p. 178.

24. E.g., *Histoire de Charles VII*, I, 62–64. "If it [the city of Rouen] had looked more maturely at its misfortune and capitulated it could have obtained from the English king terms guaranteeing its freedom and its privileges, and avoided the great calamities which it suffered." The English besieged Rouen in July 1419, and the city capitulated in January 1420.

25. Ibid., I, 44–46.

26. The capture and sack of Soissons is related in ibid., pp. 24–28.

27. Ibid., II, 42.

28. In defending human freedom as he does, Basin appeals above all to arguments taken from natural law. This type of argumentation was characteristic of much medieval juridical literature, and it extended back to the Stoics and the Church Fathers. See R. W. and A. J. Carlyle, *A History of Medieval Political Theory in the West* (London: W. Blackwood and Sons, 1936), VI, concluding chapter.

29. *Histoire de Charles VII*, II, 38–40.

30. Basin quotes the *De Officiis*, I, 4, 13; II, 7, 23–25. The Pauline references are to I Corinthians 7:23. But Basin seems somewhat embarrassed with the Pauline text: "while it is true that he counsels each Christian to remain in his walk of life . . . he does add . . . 'if you can become a freeman, take advantage of it.' "

31. *Histoire de Louis XI*, I, 177–83. Basin uses a similar dialectic to refute those who base their hostility to Joan of Arc on her evident failure, *Histoire de Charles VII*, I, 165.

32. Ibid., p. 137. *Necessitas* is a word that recurs frequently in both the *Histoire de Charles VII* and the *Histoire de Louis XI*, e.g., Book II, Chapter 3: "extrema cogente necessitate."

33. *Histoire de Charles VII*, I, 3–5. The title of this chapter is, of course, inspired by Tacitus' *sine ira et studio, Annalium Liber*, I, 1.

7   COMMYNES: HISTORY AS LOST INNOCENCE

1. C. Picqué, "Mémoire sur Philippe de Commynes," *Mémoires couronnés par l'Académie Royale de Belgique* XVI (1864):8: "Commynes est . . . le successeur de Thucydide, le précurseur de . . . Machiavel." C. A. Sainte-Beuve, *Causeries du lundi*, 7 janvier 1850 (Paris: Garnier Frères, 1857), p. 250: "[c'est] . . . notre premier historian vraiment moderne." Biographical information on Commynes is taken from J. Dufournet, *La Vie de Philippe de Commynes* (Paris: S.E.D.E.S., 1969).

2. Dufournet, *La Vie de Philippe de Commynes*, pp. 163–74.

3. Ph. de Commynes, *The Memoirs of Philippe de Commynes*, edited by S. Kinser and I. Cazeaux (Columbia, S.C.: University of South Carolina Press, 1969), I, 91 (hereafter cited as *The Memoirs*). I have adopted this translation except where I disagree with it. I have frequently cited the original in order to clarify the discussion. Original citations are from Ph. de Commynes, *Mémoires*, edited by J. Calmette and G. Durville (Paris: H. Champion, 1924–25), 2 vols. (hereafter cited as *Mémoires*).

4. *Mémoires*, II, 158: "Pour retourner à ma matière principale. . . . Pour toujours continuer ma matière."

5. *Mémoires*, I, 189–90 (my translation): "Qui eust peü prendre partie des condicions du roy nostre maistre et partie des siennes, on eust bien fait ung prince parfait." The Kinser-Cazeaux translation fails to convey the mental activity implied by the verb *prendre*.

6. *The Memoirs*, I, 335.

7. Ibid., p. 326.

8. Ibid., p. 233.

9. *Mémoires*, I, 129–30.

10. *The Memoirs*, I, 108.

11. Ibid., p. 181.

12. E.g., this moral sketch of the duke of Burgundy (*Mémoires*, I, 152): "Le duc de Bourgogne n'avoit point de faulte de hardiesse, mais bien aucunes fois faulte d'ordre." Cf. this sketch of Duke Charles of Brittany, King Louis's brother (ibid., p. 170): "Ledict Monsr Charles estoit homme qui peü ou riens faisoit de luy, mais en toutes choses estoit manyé et conduyt par autres." Commynes's portrait of Louis XI (I, 67–68) is entirely devoid of visual elements and is a cognitive interpretation of the king's moral makeup.

13. *The Memoirs*, I, 192–93.

14. Ibid., p. 356.

15. *Mémoires*, I, 157: "Et fusmes l'espace de plus de deux patenostres avant que ces archiers peüssent saillir." The time "wasted" by Charles VIII during his Italian expedition was also essentially linear (and nonprofitable): "depuis qu'il entre à Napples jusques il en partir, ne pensa que à passer temps, et d'aultre à prendre et prouffiter, mais son eage l'excusoit" (ibid., III, 134).

16. *The Memoirs*, I, 210.

17. Ibid., p. 91.

18. One of the rare instances when Commynes associates a state of consciousness with a *locus* is contained in his reminiscence of the way he felt at the battle of Montlhéry (ibid., p. 108): "I was with him all during that day and experienced less fear than I have ever felt in any place where I have ever been since."

19. Ibid., p. 258. Cf., by contrast, Commynes's description of the inexperienced English soldiers of 1477: "they were not the English who had lived in his [Charles of Burgundy's] father's time and who had taken part in the old wars with France, but these were all inexperienced men" (ibid., p. 256).

20. Ibid., p. 209.

21. *Mémoires*, I, 189: "La hayne ne diminuait point entre le roy et le duc de Bourgogne, mais toujours continua."

22. Ibid., p. 181.

23. Ibid., p. 245.

24. *The Memoirs*, I, 204.

25. Ibid., p. 325. Louis XI's cruelty right before his death "estoit mauvais signe de longue durée" (*Mémoires*, II, 154).

26. Most of Commynes's characters (save, perhaps, the author himself in his later years and minor figures like the hermit Saint François de Paule) have no authentic religious life, though they are riddled with superstitions.

27. *The Memoirs*, I, 95. One might literally translate "au saillir de mon enfance," by "when I erupted from my childhood." Cf. the use of *saillie* as a surprise attempt to break out of a trap (*Mémoires*, I, 154): "Les Liégeois . . . se libererent de faire une grosse *saillie.*"

28. *The Memoirs*, I, 238. Cf. Louis XI's sudden, unpredictable decision to put an end to Charles the Bold (*Mémoires*, I, 171): "L'an mil IIIIC LXX print vouloir au roy de se venger du duc de Bourgogne, et luy sembla qu'il en estoit heure."

29. *The Memoirs*, I, 285.

30. Ibid., p. 92.

31. Ibid., p. 302.

32. Ibid., p. 137.

33. *Mémoires*, II, 129.

34. *The Memoirs*, I, 326 (*Mémoires*, II, 157–58).

35. *Mémoires*, II, 155.

36. For indications of themes such as *fuite, diminucion, perte, délaissement, mutacion*, see *Mémoires*, I, 207 ("mutacions de ce monde"); I, 209 ("les choses de ce monde sont peu estables"); II, 105 ("il perdit honneur et chevance"); II, 87 ("il . . . estoit *eslongué* de la grace de Dieu . . . après les grandes prosperitéz, tumbent en adversitéz").

37. *The Memoirs*, I, 168.

38. Ibid., p. 132 (*Mémoires*, I, 70).

39. Ibid., p. 161 (*Mémoires*, I, 115).

40. Ibid., p. 123 (*Mémoires*, I, 54).

41. *Mémoires,* II, 224. Cf. p. 236, where "faulte de foy" is spoken of as the root of divine punishment, war, mortality, famine.

42. Ibid., I, 91. I. Cazeaux (*The Memoirs,* I, 143) translates *division* as *dissension* and fails thereby to connote the active significance of *division.*

43. Kinser-Sazeaux, *The Memoirs,* I, 150.

44. Ibid.

45. Ibid., p. 355.

46. Ibid., pp. 129–30 (*Mémoires,* I, 66).

47. *Mémoires,* II, 340–41 (my translation).

48. *The Memoirs,* I, 145 (*Mémoires,* I, 93).

49. Augustine, *Confessions,* X, 27.

50. *The Memoirs,* I, 205.

51. For a documented account of Commynes's disgrace after the death of Louis XI and his subsequent imprisonment see Dufournet, *La Vie de Philippe de Commynes,* pp. 163–74. On the possibility of a religious conversion as a result of his imprisonment see *The Memoirs,* I, 13–16.

52. *The Memoirs,* I, 145.

53. Ibid., p. 313.

54. *Mémoires,* II, 341 (my translation).

55. *The Memoirs,* I, 355 (*Mémoires,* II, 211–12).

56. P. Archambault, "Commynes's Saigesse and the Renaissance Idea of Wisdom," *Bibliothèque d'Humanisme et Renaissance* XXIX (1967):613–32, esp. 626.

57. *The Memoirs,* I, 92 (*Mémoires,* I, 3).

58. *Mémoires,* II, 156. This and the following paragraph closely follow my article, "Thucydides in France: The Notion of Justice in the *Mémoires* of Philippe de Commynes," *Journal of the History of Ideas* XXVIII, No. 1 (January 1967):89–92.

59. *The Memoirs,* I, 353.

60. Jean Dufournet, *La Destruction des mythes dans les Mémoires de Ph. de Commynes* (Geneva: Droz, 1966), p. 698: "il nous livre, tout autant qu'un récit historique, un plai doyer et, partant, un réquisitoire."

CONCLUSION: TWO STYLES

1. Froissart, *Chroniques,* II, 4.

2. E. Auerbach, *Mimesis,* translated by W. Trask (Princeton: Princeton University Press, 1953), p. 19.

3. Ibid., pp. 14–17.

4. What Auerbach (p. 19) calls the two "basic types" of representation in the Western literary tradition is a good illustration of this opposition.

5. R. L. Kilgour, *The Decline of Chivalry* (Cambridge, Mass.: Harvard University Press, 1937), p. 3.

BIBLIOGRAPHY

THIS bibliography is limited to editions and works that were consulted in the preparation of this book. Readers wishing more complete bibliographical information should consult the titles marked with an asterisk.

Texts and Translations

Basin, Thomas. *Histoire des règnes de Charles VII et de Louis XI.* 4 vols. Edited by J. Quicherat. Paris: J. Renouard, 1855–59.

——. *Histoire de Charles VII.* 2 vols. Edited by Charles Samaran. Paris: Les Belles Lettres, 1933–44.

——. *Histoire de Louis XI.* 2 vols. Edited by Charles Samaran. Paris: Les Belles Lettres, 1963–66.

Chastellain, Georges. *Oeuvres de Georges Chastellain.* 8 vols. Edited by Kervyn de Lettenhove. Brussels: Heussner, 1863–66.

——. *Oeuvres historiques inédites de Georges Chastellain.* Edited by J. A. C. Buchon. Paris: Desrez, 1883.

Clari, Robert de. *La Conquête de Constantinople.* Edited by Philippe Lauer. Paris: H. Champion, 1924.

——. *The Conquest of Constantinople.* Edited and translated by E. H. McNeal. New York: Columbia University Press, 1939.

Commynes, Philippe de. *Mémoires.* 3 vols. Edited by Mille. Dupont. Paris: Renouard, 1840–47.

——. * *Mémoires.* 2 vols. Edited by J. Calmette and G. Durville. Paris: H. Champion, 1924–25.

——. * *The Memoirs of Philippe de Commynes.* Edited by S. Kinser and translated by I. Cazeaux. Columbia, S.C.: University of South Carolina Press, 1969 (volume one of a projected two-volume translation, with an introduction by S. Kinser).

Froissart, Sire Jean. *Le Premier (-le quart) volume de Froissart des croniques de France, d'Engleterre, d'Escoce, d'Espaigne, de Bretaigne, de Gascongne, de Flanders et lieux circonvoisins.* 2 vols. in folio. Paris: M. Le Noir, 1505.

——. *Les Chroniques de sire Jean Froissart.* 3 vols. Edited by J. A. C. Buchon. Paris: A. Desrez, 1835.

——. *Oeuvres de Froissart.* 29 vols. Edited by Kervyn de Lettenhove. Brussels: V. Devaux, 1867–77.

——. *Chroniques de Jean Froissart.* Edited by Siméon Luce and G. Raynaud. Paris: J. Renouard, 1869–1957 (thirteen volumes of an unfinished edition).

Joinville, Jean, Sire de. *Histoire de Saint Louis, credo et lettre à Louis X.* Edited by Natalis de Wailly. Paris: J. Renouard, 1874; New York: Johnson Reprint Corporation, 1965.

——. *Joinville and Villehardouin: Chronicles of the Crusades.* Translated by M. R. B. Shaw. London: Penguin Books, 1963 (a good general introduction, pp. 7–25).

——. *The History of Saint Louis.* Translated by Joan Evans. London: Oxford University Press, 1938.

——. *The Life of Saint Louis.* Translated by René Hague. New York and London: Sheed and Ward, 1955.

——. *Text and Iconography for Joinville's Credo.* Edited by Lionel J. Friedman. Cambridge, Mass.: Medieval Academy of America, 1958.

La Marche, Olivier de. * *Mémoires d'Olivier de la Marche.* 4 vols. Edited by Henri Beaune and J. d'Arbaumont. Paris: H. Loones, 1883–88.

Molinet, Jean. *Chroniques de Molinet.* 3 vols. Edited by Georges Doutrepont and Omer Jodogne. Brussels: Palais de l'Académie, 1935–37.

Paris, Gaston, and Jeanroy, Alfred, editors. *Extraits des chroniqueurs français: Villehardouin, Joinville, Froissart, Commines.* Paris: Hachette, 1892.

Pauphilet, A., and Pognon, E. *Historiens et chroniqueurs du moyen âge: Robert de Clari, Villehardouin, Joinville, Froissart, Commynes.* Paris: Gallimard ("La Pléiade"), 1952.

Villehardouin, Geoffroy de. * *La Conquête de Constantinople.* 2 vols. Edited by E. Faral. Paris: Les Belles Lettres, 1938–39.

Critical and Historical Works

Alphandéry, Paul. *La Chrétienté et l'idée de croisade.* 2 vols. Paris: A. Michel, 1954.

Archambault, Paul. "The Analogy of the Body in Renaissance Political Literature." *Bibliothèque d'Humanisme et Renaissance* XXIX (January 1967):21–53.

―――. "Commynes' *Saigesse* and the Renaissance Idea of Wisdom." *Bibliothèque d'Humanisme et Renaissance* XXIX (December 1967):613–32.

―――. * "The Mémoires of Philippe de Commynes as a Manual of Political Philosophy." Ph. D. dissertation, Yale University, 1963.

―――. "Sallust in France: Thomas Basin's Idea of History and of the Human Condition." *Papers on Language and Literature* IV, 3 (1968):227–57.

―――. "Thucydides in France: The Notion of 'Justice' in the *Mémoires* of Philippe de Commynes." *Journal of the History of Ideas* XXVIII, 1 (1967): 89–98.

Aristotle. *The Basic Works of Aristotle.* Edited by Richard McKeon. New York: Random House, 1941.

Auerbach, Erich. *Mimesis: The Representation of Reality in Western Literature.* Translated by Willard Trask. Garden City, N.Y.: Doubleday, 1953.

Barnes, Harry E. *A History of Historical Writing.* 2nd. rev. ed. New York: Dover Publications, 1962.

Bernheimer, Richard. *Wild Men in the Middle Ages. A Study in Art, Sentiment, and Demonology.* Cambridge, Mass.: Harvard University Press, 1953.

Bittmann, Karl. *Ludwig XI. und Karl der Kühne. Die Memoiren des Philippe de Commynes als historische Quelle.* 2 vols. Göttingen: Vandenhoeck and Ruprecht, 1964–70.

Bloch, Marc. *Feudal Society.* Translated by L. A. Manyon. Chicago: University of Chicago Press, 1961.

Born, L. K. "The Perfect Prince: A Study in Thirteenth- and Fourteenth-Century Ideals." *Speculum* III (1928).

Bossuat, R., Pichard, Msgr. L., Raynaud de Lage, editors. *Dictionnaire des lettres françaises: le moyen âge.* Paris: A. Fayard, 1964.

Bouwsma, William J. "The Politics of Commynes." *The Journal of Modern History* XXIII (December 1951):315–28.

Boysen, A. R. *Ueber den Begriff preu im Französischen* (*preu, prou, prouesse, prud'homme, prud'homie, prude, pruderie*). Inaugural-Dissertation, Westfälische Wilhelms-Universität zu Munster. Lengerich, 1941.

Brandt, W. J. *The Shape of Medieval History: Studies in Modes of Perception*. New Haven: Yale University Press, 1966.

Brault, Gérard J. *Early Blazon. Heraldic Terminology in the Twelfth and Thirteenth Centuries with Special Reference to Arthurian Literature*. Oxford: Clarendon Press, 1972.

Bridge, J. S. C. *A History of France from the Death of Louis XI*. 5 vols. Oxford: Clarendon Press, 1921–36.

Burgess, G. S. *Contribution à l'étude du vocabulaire pré-courtois. Publications Romanes et Françaises*, 110. Geneva: Droz, 1970.

Calmette, Joseph. *Les Grands ducs de Bourgogne*. Paris: A. Michel, 1949.

Carlyle, R. W. and A. J. *A History of Medieval Political Theory in the West*. 6 vols. London: W. Blackwood and Sons, 1903–36.

Cicero, Marcus T. *De Officiis*. Edited by T. E. Page. London: W. Heinemann, 1928.

Debidour, Antonin. *Les Chroniqueurs, première série. Villehardouin, Joinville*. Paris: H. Lecène et H. Oudin, 1888.

———. *Les Chroniqueurs, deuxième série. Froissart, Commines*. Paris: H. Lecène et H. Oudin, 1890.

———. *Les Chroniqueurs français du moyen âge. Etudes, analyses, et extraits*. Paris: Lecène, Oudin, 1895 (edited in collaboration with E. Etienne).

Delaborde, Henri-F. *L'Expédition de Charles VIII en Italie*. Paris: Firmin-Didiot, 1888.

———. *Jean de Joinville et les seigneurs de Joinville, suivi d'un catalogue de leurs actes*. Paris: Picard et fils, 1894.

Delachenal, Roland, editor. *Les Grandes chroniques de France. Chronique des règnes de Jean II et de Charles V*. Paris: Société de l'histoire de France, 1920.

De Lubac, Henri de. *Exégèse médiévale*. 4 vols. Paris: Aubier, 1959–64.

Doutrepont, Georges. *La Littérature française à la cour des ducs de Bourgogne*. Paris: H. Champion, 1909.

Dufournet, Jean. *La Destruction des mythes dans les Mémoires de Ph. de Commynes*. Geneva: Droz, 1966.

———. *La Vie de Philippe de Commynes*. Paris: S.E.D.E.S., 1969.

Faral, Edmond, "Geoffroy de Villehardouin: la question de sa sincérité." *Revue Historique* CLXVII (1936):530–82.

Fortescue, Sir John. *The Governance of England*. Edited by C. Plummer. Oxford: Clarendon Press, 1885.

———. *De Laudibus Legum Anglie*. Edited by S. B. Chrimes. Cambridge: The University Press, 1942.

Foulet, Alfred. "Joinville." *Romanic Review* (1941):233–43.

Frappier, Jean. "Le Style de Villehardouin dans les discours de sa chronique." *Bulletin of the John Rylands Library,* Manchester XXX (1946): 57–70.

Frolow, A. *Recherches sur la déviation de la IVe Croisade.* Paris: Presses Universitaires de France, 1955.

Funck-Brentano, Frantz. *Féodalité et chevalerie.* Paris: Editions de Paris, 1946.

———. *Le Moyen âge.* Paris: Hachette, 1951.

Gilbert, A. H. *Machiavelli's Prince and Its Forerunners.* Chapel Hill: University of North Carolina Press, 1938.

Gilson, Etienne. *History of Christian Philosophy in the Middle Ages.* New York: Random House, 1955.

———. *History of Philosophy and Philosophical Education.* Milwaukee: Marquette University Press, 1948.

———. *Réalisme thomiste et critique de la connaissance.* Paris: J. Vrin, 1939.

Goldin, Frederick R. * "The Mirror and the Image in Medieval Courtly Literature." Ph.D. dissertation, Columbia University, 1964.

Gougenheim, G. "Notes sur le vocabulaire de Clari et de Villehardouin." *Romania* LXVIII (1944–45):401–21.

Gutsch, Milton R. "A Twelfth-Century Preacher—Fulk of Neuilly." In *The Crusades,* edited by Louis J. Paetow. New York: Columbia University Press, 1928.

Hanning, Robert. *The Vision of History in Early Britain: From Gildas to Geoffrey of Monmouth.* New York: Columbia University Press, 1966.

Hay, Denys. *The Medieval Centuries.* London: Methuen, 1964.

Heckscher, W. S. "Bernini's Elephant and Obelisk." *Art Bulletin* XXIX (1947):158–65.

Howard, Donald. *The Three Temptations: Medieval Man in Search of the World.* Princeton: Princeton University Press, 1966.

Huizinga, Jean. *Le Déclin du moyen âge.* Translated by Julia Bastin. Paris: Payot, 1967.

Jacob, Ernest F. *The Fifteenth Century, 1399–1485.* Oxford: Clarendon Press, 1961.

———. *Essays in Later Medieval History.* Manchester: Manchester University Press; New York: Barnes and Noble, 1968.

Kendall, Paul M. * *Louis XI.* New York: W. Norton, 1971.

Kilgour, R. L. *The Decline of Chivalry.* Cambridge, Mass.: Harvard University Press, 1937.

Krey, A. C. "The Making of an Historian in the Middle Ages." *Speculum* XVI (1941):149 sq.

Lavisse, Ernest. * *Histoire de France. Depuis les origines jusqu'à la révolution.*

——. *Tome III, première partie. Louis VII Philippe Auguste—Louis VIII.* Paris: Hachette, 1911.

——. *Tome III, deuxième partie. Saint Louis—Philippe le Bel—Les Derniers Capétiens directs* (1226–1328). Paris: Hachette, 1901.

——. *Tome IV, première partie. Les Premiers Valois et la querre de cent ans* (1328–1422). Paris: Hachette, 1902.

——. *Tome IV, deuxième partie. Charles VII, Louis XI et les premières années de Charles VIII.* Paris: Hachette, 1902.

Leeman, A. D. *Orationis Ratio: The Stylistic Theories and Practice of the Roman Orators, Historians and Philosophers.* Amsterdam: A. M. Hakkert, 1963.

Lejeune-Dehousse, Rita. *Recherches sur le thème: les chansons de geste et l'histoire.* Liège: Faculté des Lettres et Sciences, 1948.

Lewis, D. B. W. *King Spider; Some Aspects of Louis XI of France and his Companions.* New York: Coward-McCann, 1929.

Lewis, Peter S. *Later Medieval France: The Polity.* New York: St. Martin's Press, 1968.

Longnon, Jean. *Recherches sur la vie de Geoffroy de Villehardouin.* Paris: H. Champion, 1939.

Machiavelli, N. *Il principe.* Edited by L. A. Burd. Oxford: Clarendon Press, 1891.

McNeal, E. H. "Chronicler and Conte: A Note on Narrative Style in G. of Villehardouin and R. de Clari." *Festschrift für M. Blakeman Evans.* Columbus: Ohio State University Press, 1945.

McRobbie, Kenneth. "The Concept of Advancement in the Fourteenth Century." *The Canadian Journal of History* VI, 1 (March 1971):1–19.

——. "Woman and Love: Some Aspects of Competition in Late Medieval Society." *Mosaic* V, 2 (Winter 1971–72):139–68.

Molinier, Auguste. * *Les Sources de l'histoire de France des origines aux querres d'Italie* (1494). 6 vols. Paris: A. Picard et fils, 1901–1906.

Muratori, L. A. *Rerum Italicarum Scriptores.* 25 vols. Milan: F. Argellati, 1723–51.

Neff, Wilfrid B. *The Moral Language of Philippe de Commynes.* New York: Columbia University Press, 1937.

Newhall, R. A. *The English Conquest of Normandy, 1416–1424.* New Haven: Yale University Press, 1924.

Painter, Sydney. *French Chivalry.* Baltimore: The Johns Hopkins Press, 1940.

Patch, Howard R. *The Goddess Fortuna in Medieval Literature.* Cambridge, Mass.: Harvard University Press, 1927.

Pauphilet, Albert. *Le Legs du moyen âge.* Melun: d'Argences, 1950.

Pears, Edwin. *The Fall of Constantinople*. New York: Longmans, 1885.

Penwarden, P. J. "A Linguistic and Stylistic Comparison of the Chronicles by Villehardouin and R. de Clari." Ph.D. dissertation, University of London, 1953.

Pérouse, Gabriel. "Georges Chastellain, Etude sur l'histoire politique et littéraire du XVe siècle." *Mémoires de l'Académie royale de Belgique*, 2e série (VII), 1910.

Perroy, Edouard. *La Guerre de cent ans*. Paris: Gallimard, 1946.

Picqué, Camille. "Mémoire sur Philippe de Commynes." *Mémoires couronnés par l'Académie royale de Belgique* XVI (1864).

Poole, R. L. *Chronicles and Annals: A Brief Outline of their Origin and Growth*. Oxford: Clarendon Press, 1926.

Poulet, Georges. *L'Espace proustien*. Paris: Gallimard, 1963.

——. *Etudes sur le temps humain*, I. Paris: Plon, 1949.

Queller, D. E., and Stratton, S. J. "A Century of Controversy on the Fourth Crusade." In *Studies in Medieval and Renaissance History*. Edited by William M. Bowsky (Lincoln: University of Nebraska Press, 1959), pp. 235–77.

Rice, E. F. *The Renaissance Idea of Wisdom*. Cambridge, Mass.: Harvard University Press, 1958.

Rousset, Paul. *Histoire des croisades*. Paris: Payot, 1957.

——. "Un problème de méthodologie: l'événement et sa perception." *Mélanges offerts à René Crozet*. Edited by P. Gallais and Y. J. Rion. Poitiers: Publ. du C.E.S.C.M., 1966.

Runciman, Sir Stephen. *Byzantine Civilization*. New York: Longmans, Green, 1933.

——. *The Eastern Schism: A Study of the Papacy and the Eastern Churches During the XIth and XIIth Centuries*. Oxford: Clarendon Press, 1956.

——. *A History of the Crusades*. Cambridge: The University Press, 1954.

Rutebeuf. *Oeuvres complètes de Rutebeuf*. 2 vols. Edited by E. Faral and J. Bastin. Paris: A. et J. Picard, 1959–60.

Sainte-Beuve, C. A. "G. de Villehardouin." *Causeries du lundi*, IX, 3rd ed. Paris: Garnier frères, 1857.

——. "Philippe de Commynes." *Causeries du lundi*, 7 janv. 1850, Paris: Garnier frères, 1857.

Saint-Pathus, Guillaume de. *Vie de Saint Louis*. Paris: A. Picard et fils, 1899.

Sallust. *De Coniuratione Catilinae*. In *Salluste*, edited by A. Ernout. Paris: Les Belles Lettres, 1946.

Sayers, W. J. S. "The Beginnings and Early Development of Old French

Historiography." Ph.D. dissertation, University of California at Berkeley, 1966.

Shears, F. S. *Froissart: Chronicler and Poet*. London: G. Routledge and Sons, 1930.

Shotwell, James T. *The History of History*. Rev. ed. New York: Columbia University Press, 1939.

Southern, R. W. *The Making of the Middle Ages*. New Haven: Yale University Press, 1953.

Tessier, Jules. *La Quatrième croisade: la diversion sur Zara et Constantinople*. Paris: E. Leroux, 1884.

Thomas Aquinas, St. *Selected Political Writings*. Edited by A. P. d'Entrèves. Oxford: Clarendon Press, 1948.

Tillich, Paul. *The New Being*. New York: Scribner, 1955.

Van der Haeghen, Ph. "Examen des droits de Charles VIII sur le royaume de Naples." *Revue Historique* XXVIII (1885):89–111.

Vasiliev, A. A. *History of the Byzantine Empire*. 2 vols. Madison: University of Wisconsin Press, 1961.

White, Lynn. *Medieval Technology and Social Change*. Oxford: Clarendon Press, 1962.

Whitehead, A. N. *Modes of Thought*. New York: Macmillan, 1938.

Whiting, B. J. "Froissart as Poet." *Medieval Studies* VIII (1946):189–216.

Williamson, G. H., translator and editor. Eusebius. *The History of the Church from Christ to Constantine*. New York: New York University Press, 1966.

INDEX

Acroistre, accretion, theme in Commynes's *Memoirs*, 110–11

Ages of the world (*aetates mundi*), analogy with ages of man, 3–5

Agincourt, battle of: 14, 17, 20, 87; in Basin's chronicle, 92–93, 96; Basin's interpretation of, 95

Alexander, conquests of, 1

Angelus, Alexius (Alexius IV of Constantinople), 8–10, 25–27, 33. *See also* Fourth Crusade, Villehardouin

Anjou, Charles of (Duke): brother to Saint Louis, 11; hostility to Frederick II's descendants, 12; campaign in Sicily, 102

Aristotle, 2, 50, 102–103, 122

Armagnacs. *See* Orléans, House of

Aubigné, Agrippa d', universal chronicle not in medieval tradition, 125 n.5

Auerbach, Erich, description of basic styles, 120

Augustine, Saint (bishop of Hippo): chronological system of, 3–4; influence on medieval historiography, 4; decline of influence, 5; social vision, 48–49; Commynes echoes themes of, 111; importance of his *De Genesi*, 125 n.4, 125 n.5

Augustus, Caesar, reign of, 1

Baldwin of Flanders: proclaimed Latin emperor of the East, 10; dispute with Boniface of Montferrat, 26, 38. *See also* Villehardouin

Bascot de Mauléon, typical Froissart figure, 71, 121

Basin, Thomas: compared with Commynes, 23–24; trained as classical humanist, 24; conception of historiography, 87–99; life, 87–88; focusing, selection, intelligibility in chronicle of, 88–90; creates dynamic characters, 91–93; considers history intelligible texture, 94–96; universal scope of, 97–99; on basic style, 217–23 *passim. See also* Charles VII, Louis XI

Bavaria, Isabella of, marriage to Charles VI of France, 18, 61–62

Beauvais, Vincent of, chronicle written in Augustinian tradition, 4, 125 n.5

Beaulieu, Geoffroy de, biography of Saint Louis, 129 n.2

Bede, Venerable, adopts Augustinian analogies, 4

Bedford, Duke of: death, 20; alliance with Philip of Burgundy, 21